From Aspiration to Reality: Balancing the Elements

Lyn Fernandez

From Aspiration to Reality: Balancing the Elements © 2024 Lyn Fernandez

Dedication

"To all of you who dare to dream and bring this dream to reality, may the pages of this book inspire and guide you through your journey."

Contents

Gratitude

Acknowledgments

From Aspiration to Reality: Balancing the Elements!

I've been journaling since 1998 and I am amazed at the contents of these journals... my experiences, good and not too good, happy and sad, boldness and fear, ups and downs, love and hate. In a big way, it is therapeutic and allows me to reflect on my journey as a mother, a nurse, a wife, a friend, a Feng Shui Consultant and Practitioner. This is also my way of celebrating my accomplishments and navigating the challenges and trials that came with the package. My daily journaling allowed me to discover myself, leading to self-awareness and of what I aspire for and want in life. It gave me the freedom to express myself and go after what I want. First, it was written on paper, then it was put into action. This is a compilation of my life's yins and yangs and it's still going...

Gratitude to Father Azam for his story in the "Knowledge, Self-cultivation, Spirituality and Wisdom" portion of the book. He is my favorite priest in our parish because of how he engages with the parishioners by telling personal stories backdropping with biblical references.

He also comes down from the altar when giving his sermons to get closer to the people. I see people's faces beam when they see him getting ready for his church services.

Gratitude to Chrislei Shaw for her story in the "Knowledge, Self-cultivation and Spirituality" portion of the book. She practices yoga and she thirsts for knowledge and applies it to her life.

Gratitude to Elizabeth Manalo, for her stories in the "Career" and "Helpful People" portions of the book. She tells us about her challenges and obstacles in her practice as a Doctor of Physical Therapy and how she overcame them, eventually leading to her success.

Gratitude to Pharisiah Gail, for her insight and solutions to common "Love and Relationships" challenges and problems. She is an inspirational author of two books, "Daily Dose of Sunshine" and "Choose to Rise".

Gratitude to Grace Hoversholm, for her story in the "Family" portion of the book. She is a military veteran married to another military serviceman and a mother of two beautiful girls. She talked about her love for family, her parents, and her siblings as well as the challenges and the lessons she learned growing up that helped her navigate her way to becoming a great wife to her husband and a great mother to her girls without losing herself and identity in the process.

Gratitude to Minnie Ogirala, for her story in the "Family" portion of the book. Minnie is the mother of two very accomplished daughters. She said that she is grateful for the lessons that she learned from her parents and humbly wonders if she has done well passing the wisdom that she learned to her daughters.

Gratitude to Jocelyn Francisco for her stories in the "Family and Culture", "Children and Creativity" and "Fame and Reputation" portions of the book. She is a Clinical Psychologist and an author of children's books. She joyfully sums it up by saying that becoming a parent is her greatest adventure.

Gratitude to Mina Urbino, for her story in the "Wealth and Prosperity" portion of the book. She is a retired Registered Nurse and volunteers her time at her parish church. She is now enjoying her financial freedom because of how well she managed her financial challenges and risks.

I am grateful to Chloe Edge, my initially Hatha Yoga instructor, who later became my writing instructor and mentor and then introduced me to the Al-Anon Family Groups at the time that I needed it most in my life. Her story in the "Meditation and Well-being" portion of the book is incredible. She also helps me be flexible in body, mind, and spirit.

Gratitude to Bianca Pace, for her story in the "Children and Creativity" portion of the book. Bianca is a military servicewoman married to another military serviceman. She is the mother of four-year-old AJ and two-year-old Chloe. Her work as a military personnel is outstanding. She also says that parenting means she has to reconcile between raising children and her relationship with her husband.

Gratitude to Raelyn Fernandez for her story in the "Children and Creativity" portion of the book. She is a stay- at-home mother of five and a half year old Abram and fifteen month old Micah and says that she tries to balance her inner creativity and those of her sons' and still remain on top of the game.

Gratitude to Virginia Agcayab for her story in the "Fame and Reputation" portion of the book. She is a Marriage, Family, and Child Counselor (MFCC). She said her challenge is that she is a marriage and family therapist, but she is not married and doesn't have kids. But she has been a spiritual mother for a lot of these kids and a mother figure for a lot of those kids' parents. Now, she is parenting her own mother.

I am grateful to my husband, Rey, who gave me the space and guidance to bring this book to fruition.

Everyone has his/her aspirations in life. We just have to trust ourselves, our abilities, and the universe. If we have the right intentions and work toward those intentions, our aspirations will become reality.

Ask and you shall receive!

Introduction

I started my Feng Shui studies in the early 2000s. I became a Feng Shui Consultant in 2003 after following Master Peter Leung in the Classical School of Feng Shui and Chinese Metaphysics, as well as Four Pillars of Destiny or BaZi. I also had my day and main job as a Registered Nurse. So, I worked as a Registered Nurse and also read birthdays, homes, and businesses for a while.

I went on to further my Feng Shui studies with Terah Collins as my teacher, in the Western School of Feng Shui, as well as Feng Shui Design at the Sheffield School of Interior Design.

Before my Feng Shui studies, I had some ideas about what to do to attain these aspirations, but they were foggy, piecemeal, and not sincere. I was born in the Philippines and had heard about feng shui, but I was not that interested at that time. I heard them call it "Fung Suy."

My favorite and only cure that I knew was the round multi-faceted crystal. But, is crystal the only answer and solution to every feng shui challenge?

As an adult, my interest in feng shui grew because of the common sense that I saw in this ancient practice.

I started writing articles shortly after I formally finished my feng shui studies and I wanted to continue writing these articles, but somehow, it turned into a book.

I retired from nursing in 2022, and I thought that was my "someday." Someday, I will travel the world with my husband. Someday, I will run my first full marathon after running several half marathons and being a Triple Crown holder. Someday, I will volunteer at my church, be a part of a ministry, and be of service to my community. Someday, I will be a part of an organization that inspires alcoholics and drug addicts to turn their lives around, find the good in themselves, and be a positive influence on people around them and the next generation. Someday!

Along the way of my feng shui journey, I met these wonderful people who I wanted to include in this book to illustrate that when you aspire, you can achieve ... sometimes right away, and sometimes, it might take a while. You just have to have the right intentions, and then, act on them.

Just like a lot of people, things were foggy in the beginning, but I continued to search for answers to what I want in life, praying and listening to my Higher Power for greater clarity.

Knowing what we want in life will give us a better understanding of what areas in our lives to work on in conjunction with what guas in our homes to activate. We are all interconnected. God places people in our lives and God places us in other people's lives for a reason. This is Divine Intervention! We all have aspirations. Everything is interconnected. We meet people on our journeys who touch us in many different ways and make us a better person.

Chapter One: The Five Areas of Influence

In the School of Chinese Metaphysics, Master Peter Leung taught us that the Chinese believe that people are affected by five areas of influence. These areas are:

1. ***Fate or Destiny:*** This is decided from the moment we take our first breath. This is determined by heaven.

2. ***Luck:*** This occurs in the form of man-made luck and heaven-luck. Man-made luck is the luck we create for ourselves and it is within our control. Heaven-luck — we have no control of this. It determines the condition of our birth, our character and our circumstances.

3. ***Feng Shui***: Choosing and creating the best environment inside and outside to optimize positive energy and minimize negative influences. Feng shui is earth-luck.

4. Good deeds and character — treating others well.

5. Education, knowledge and hard work.

Chapter Two: What is Feng Shui?

Feng Shui (Fung Shway), in essence, means "Wind and Water." Wind is the unseen and water is the seen. Everyone has aspirations in their lives (unseen), whether it is their career or life journey, self-knowledge and spirituality, love and relationships, etc. What are we willing to do (seen) to achieve these aspirations and make them our reality?

Feng Shui is often described as the ancient Chinese art of placement to create balance and harmony within ourselves and the universe to enhance our lives and the lives of the people around us.

Feng Shui is the art of designing your home and your surroundings to promote success in life, health, wealth, and happiness.

Feng Shui provides us with tools and methods to change our surroundings to achieve specific results and increase our overall well-being, happiness, and success.

Using the principles of Feng Shui, we can arrange furnishings to create a balanced and comfortable environment, which will in turn promote a balanced life.

Feng Shui connects nature to humanity.

Feng Shui makes us aware of how our surroundings affect us.

Wind and water are both carriers of ch'i (vital life force). We create heaven on earth. We make our aspirations a reality.

"The reason feng shui is becoming popular in the West is that people are beginning to realize that there are alternative ways and methods of viewing the universe, of understanding the way energy moves and works and how these energies affect our well-being (Essential Feng Shui)."

2.1   The Major Concepts of Feng Shui

1. Flow of energy – Ch'i is a vital energy force that is believed to flow through all living things and its flow is thought to influence the health, happiness, and overall well-being of individuals. By optimizing the flow of energy, feng shui aims to create a harmonious and supportive environment that enhances the lives of the people who inhabit that home.

2. The balance of yin and yang refers to the harmonious coexistence of opposing forces in the universe. Yin and yang are the two fundamental principles in ancient Chinese philosophy, describing the interconnected and interdependent nature of all things. For example, a. combining warm and cool colors. b. Mixing rounded and angular shapes.

c. Balancing soft and hard textures. d. Combining calm and energetic elements.

By achieving a balance of yin and yang, Feng Shui aims to create a supportive and nourishing environment that fosters well-being and prosperity.

3. Interaction of the five elements in the universe — This refers to the dynamic relationship among the five fundamental elements of the universe: Water, Wood, Fire, Earth, and Metal.

The goal of Feng Shui is to balance and harmonize the elements to create a supportive and nourishing environment.

By understanding and working with the interaction of the five elements, Feng Shui aims to create a harmonious and supportive environment that enhances the health, happiness, and well-being of individuals.

About four thousand years ago, there were no computers, clocks, nor digital equipment that we enjoy today. But for some reason, the farmers knew exactly when to plant their crops, and when to harvest them. People went where water was abundant for their crops. The fishermen knew when to fish by looking at the sky at night. People even knew how to tell time by using a stick. They also knew where to build their houses. They knew where to find these areas. So, back to location ... location ... location!

As unbelievable as it seems at times, people have survived for thousands of years without technology at their immediate disposal. This was possible through a connection between nature and humanity. People were in tune with nature. This connection still exists today ... though people seem to do their best, at times, to ignore it.

However, one way or another, we practice feng shui in our lives, but some don't know what to call it and sometimes they are not aware that they are doing it. For example: your teenage daughter is applying to five colleges/universities and you are praying that she gets accepted to the one that she likes most. Besides praying for her, you think you should do more. So, you start cleaning and decluttering her room. Whether you are aware or not, this action can lead you closer to the goal of her being accepted to the University of her choice.

I have always been fascinated with nature... how everything seems to be in the right place.   The great, big sky filled with stars, the sun, the moon, and all the heavenly bodies. The big bodies of water filled with all kinds of fish ...plants, and living things that can only survive in the sea. The land where humans and animals live ... trees, mountains, and hills. Have you ever wondered? Yes ... we are naturally in harmony with nature.

So, historically, people were in tune with nature. Today, people are still in tune with nature, but because of busy lives, an eat-and-run attitude, we lose touch or don't even bother realizing it, because we don't have the time.

2.2 Application of Feng Shui

"We shape our buildings; thereafter they shape us" (Winston Churchill). Before you build your house, don't you hire an architect.... a contractor? You work with these experts to help you build the house of your dreams. After building your house, you continue to keep your house up by dressing it the way you imagine it to look like. When you take care of your house, your house will take care of you. It will protect you from the sun, the rain, and the other outside elements that will harm you. This is Feng Shui, applied.

Selecting colors, materials, and furnishings is important to create a harmonious and supportive environment for you. Color is the easiest way to apply feng shui principles to your space, work, or home.

Designing outdoor spaces is also beneficial to balance energy and create a peaceful atmosphere.

By applying feng shui principles, individuals can harmonize their surroundings, improve their quality of life, and enhance their overall well-being.

Another application of Feng Shui: we aspire for better relationships with our spouse, partner, and children. We aspire for more money to send our children to college. We aspire to have someone we can count on, maybe a friend, your boss, your parish priest, your patron saint who you pray to. We aspire for knowledge and self-improvement. We aspire for better health and a better career. This is the unseen (wind). Then, we take action in response to these aspirations. Treat our loved ones better, and show them gratitude, appreciation, and respect. Go back to school and learn something that you are fascinated about. Look for a part-time job, work additional hours, or go into business and earn more money for your children's education. The actions that we take to make things better are the seen (water). We have to have a purpose in our lives.

2.3 Is feng shui a religion?

No, Feng Shui is not a religion nor a religious practice. Even if you religiously feng shui your home, your business or your life, it still does not make feng shui a religion. Although it is good to practice feng shui every day. You might find the positive change that you are looking for.

2.4 Schools of Feng Shui

There are two major schools of Feng Shui: The Classical School of Feng Shui and The Black Hat Sect School.

The Classical School of Feng Shui is the oldest school of feng shui, which was used over four thousand years ago. It is further divided into two schools, namely: The Compass School and The Form School.

In The Compass School, personal data is required to discover good directions. As its name says, you need a compass for everything. What direction is your house facing? What direction is your house sitting (backing)? Depending on your birthday, what is your best and most auspicious direction?

The Form School is the first and oldest school of Classical Feng Shui ...

It uses the four celestial animals as the guideline.

The Red Phoenix is on the front of the house. This means that your front should be open and airy, and free from obstruction. You do not want a big tree in front of your door because it blocks the ch'i from coming in. You would want all the blessings that the universe can offer coming in freely. The Red Phoenix is associated with the south and the color associated with the Red Phoenix is red. This is probably why the red door is very popular.

The White Tiger is on the right side (facing your house). There should be a building on this side for protection, but the building should be lower than the building on the left side. The White Tiger is associated with the West and with the metal element. The White Tiger is believed to protect you from harm.

The Green Dragon is located on the left side (facing your house). It should be a building taller than the White Tiger. It is believed that the Green Dragon is the most powerful and protective celestial animal. It attracts wealth and luck. The Green Dragon is associated with the East. It symbolizes strength, goodness, courage, vigilance and serenity.

The Black Turtle represents longevity, strength, endurance, support and stability. It is located at the back of your home. The saying, "I got your back," applies very well here. The backing of your home can be a building, a wall, trees, or a flat hill.

According to Feng Shui, the best location for your home is in the "belly of the dragon."

This means the "armchair" position – the front is airy and bright, open space, a building on either side, and a good backing.

Black Sect School of Feng Shui: This is the newest school of feng shui. It uses the three-door approach. It uses the entrance quadrant of your home as the guideline.

The entrance quadrant of your home has the "knowledge/self-cultivation", "Career/life path", and "Helpful People/Mentors and travel" areas. Generally, the entrance is where the "Career/Life Path" area is located. The entrance can also be located at the "Knowledge, Self-cultivation, Wisdom, Spirituality" or the "Helpful People, Mentors, and Travel" areas.

Colorful doormats, attractive and different colored flowers, a fountain, and a bird bath would be a good décor for this area. Make the entrance attractive and balanced by adding the five different feng shui elemental colors to attract balance and harmony to your life.

Black Hat Sect Feng Shui is popularly known as "Western Feng Shui" in the West, wherein the practitioners analyze the house floor plan, the layout of the different rooms in the house, furniture placement, and the balancing of the five Feng Shui elements. Balancing the yin and yang of the different rooms in your home is essential to attaining harmony within the entire household.

2.5 The Nine Feng Shui Cures

Like anything else that does not always work, there are solutions! In Feng Shui, they are called cures.

1. **Lights:** Use lamps to brighten dark areas, candles make you in the mood for love, mirrors to reflect natural light, color-changing bulbs to liven a conversation, or relationship, skylight to bring in natural light. Light symbolizes awareness, understanding, and enlightenment, helping to uplift and transform energy. It activates and circulates the ch'i of space, helping to remove stagnation and promote flow. Light can improve your mood and emotions, creating a sense of warmth and comfort. Light can make a space feel larger, helping to counteract the feeling of confinement.

2. **Living things:** In feng shui, living things like plants or animals are considered powerful cures. By incorporating living things, you can enhance the energy, beauty, and life force of space, promoting harmony and well-being. Living things can absorb and emit energy, helping to balance and harmonize the environment. Put plants in areas needing

energy balance. Keeping aquariums or fish tanks to enhance wealth and prosperity. Raising pets, like dogs and cats, for companionship.

3. ***Moving objects:*** Metal or wooden wind chimes activate energy. Gentle breeze from fans can circulate energy. Hang mobiles or whirligigs with symbols or shapes that rotate or spin; fountains, aquariums or small waterfalls that create movement. They stimulate energy flow, helping to remove stagnation and promote circulation. Moving objects can disrupt stagnant energy, refreshing space. Moving objects add dynamism to space, countering static energy. Moving objects can attract and draw in positive energy. Moving objects can distract negative energy, reducing its impact.

4. ***Heavy objects:*** Large stones or boulders, heavy sculptures or statues, heavy vases and urns, thick, heavy books or bookends, metal or ceramic weights are examples of heavy objects feng shui cures. In feng shui, heavy objects ground and stabilize energy, preventing it from becoming too scattered or chaotic. Heavy objects can counteract negative energy, weighing it down and preventing it from spreading. Heavy objects provide a sense of solidity and permanence, promoting feelings of security and stability. Heavy objects can support and anchor energy, preventing it from becoming too unstable.

5. ***Hollow objects:*** Examples of hollow objects: empty vases or urns, holes or cavities in stone or crystals, bell-shaped objects or wind chimes, singing bowls or drums, and flutes. By

incorporating hollow objects as feng shui cures, you can absorb and neutralize negative energy. Hollow objects can absorb and contain negative energy, preventing it from spreading. Hollow objects can create a vacuum effect, drawing in and neutralizing negative energy. Hollow objects can amplify intentions and energies, making them more powerful. Hollow objects symbolize space, representing the potential for new possibilities and opportunities.

6. ***Electrical objects:*** Examples of electrical objects: bright lights and scones, color-changing LED lights, televisions and computers, radios, stereo systems, boombox, electrical appliances (in specific areas).By incorporating electrical objects as feng shui cures, you can activate energy, enhance brightness, and bring warmth and innovation to a space, promoting a more dynamic and vibrant environment. Electrical objects can activate and stimulate energy, helping overcome stagnation. Electrical lighting can enhance brightness, symbolizing clarity and awareness. Electrical objects represent the fire element, bringing warmth and energy to space. Electrical objects can improve energy circulation, helping overcome blockages. Electrical objects symbolize innovation, progress, and modernization.

7. ***Colors:*** Colors can activate specific areas of life, for example, red for relationships, green for wealth, yellow for wisdom and happiness. Colors can balance and harmonize energy, counteracting excessive or deficient energy.

Colors can influence mood and emotions, promoting relaxation, calmness or energy. Colors symbolize intentions and energies, manifesting desired outcomes. By incorporating colors as feng shui cures, particularly when used in conjunction with the five feng shui elements, you can balance energy, enhance mood, and manifest intentions, promoting a more harmonious and supportive environment.

8. ***Sounds:*** By incorporating sounds as feng shui cures, you can activate energy, clear negative energy, balance elements, and manifest intentions, promoting a more harmonious and supportive environment. Sounds can activate and stimulate energy, helping to overcome stagnation. Sounds can clear and dispel negative energy, promoting a fresh start. Specific sounds can balance the elements, restoring harmony. Sounds can influence mood and emotions. Sounds can symbolize intentions and manifest desired outcomes.
Common sound cures: A ringing bell can clarify and purify a manifestation. Wind chimes promote balance, harmony and relaxation. Drum sounds can promote energy, vitality and protection. Gongs are for healing, transformation and medit.

9. ***Intuition:*** This is a powerful tool that helps you navigate and balance your energy and space with inner wisdom and guidance. Trusting your intuition helps tap into your inner wisdom, guiding you to make decisions that align with your energy and space. For example, you thought the green Buddha statue

looked good in the far left corner of your living room. You accidentally activated your wealth corner! So, if you win the lottery after that action, act pleasantly surprised. There is a connection! It pays to follow your intuition in this way. Intuition can help sense energy imbalances or blockages, allowing you to address them. Intuition guides decision-making, ensuring that changes and adjustments align with your goals and energy. Intuition builds trust in your inner guidance, allowing you to confidently make changes and adjustments.

2.6 *Feng Shui Challenges and Cures*

In Feng Shui, we try to create heaven on earth. Humans are considered the connectors of heaven and earth and are here to bring ideas from heaven into reality through intention + action and emotion.

Challenge: Messy entry way. A messy entryway can put you in a bad mood and can cause accidents.

Cure: Put stuff in storage boxes, live plants, good cleaning and decluttering habits, attractive artwork.

Challenge: The main entrance door directly faces the stairs. The up and down energy can cause your luck to be scattered and unstable.

Cure: Place a curtain, screen, plant, or furniture in between the door and the stairs.

Challenge: Stairs in the center of the house. The stairs at the center of the house can cause health issues. It can also reduce wealth, luck, or fortune.

Cure: Hang a crystal to slow down the ch'i.

Challenge: Kitchen faucet directly facing a stove. This can cause disharmony, arguments, and conflict.

Cure: Relocate the faucet or stove so that they are not facing each other, or put a plant or anything of the wood element between the stove and the faucet.

Challenge: The kitchen stove can be seen from the main entrance. This can cause difficulty in saving money.

Cure: Place a door, furniture, curtain, screen, or big plants to block the view.

Challenge: Ceiling beams directly above a sofa, desk, or bed. This can cause stress and a sense of oppression.

Cure: Move the sofa, desk or bed away from the beam, cover the beam or add a ceiling design to hide the beam or hang a crystal.

Challenge: Desk facing a wall. This can cause a symbol of a dark future and no possibilities.

Cure: Relocate the desk. If this is not possible, add a painting of a beautiful landscape or a mirror on the wall so you can see behind you.

Challenge: The mirror faces a bed directly. This can cause the ch'i to be scattered easily and make it hard for the person to rest and relax.

Cure: Relocate the mirror so that it is not directly facing the bed, or cover the mirror with fabric at night.

Challenge: The bedroom is located above a garage or a space. This can cause a feeling of instability.

Cure: Four elephant figurines symbolizing weight for groundedness, or move the bed to a different location.

Challenge: The restroom door directly facing a bedroom or a bed. This can cause health issues.

Cure: Place a curtain or a screen between the bed and the bathroom door. You can also place plants between the bed and the bathroom door.

Chapter Three: What is ch'i?

Ch'i is the vital life force that is present in us and flows through us and through everything.

Different cultures call it differently:

1. The Christians call it Christ.

2. The Catholics call it Spirit.

3. The Japanese call it Ki.

4. The Hindus call it Prana.

5. The Greeks call it Pneuma.

6. The Hebrews call it Ruah

It is the one that is present in our body's system. If we treat our body right – proper diet, and exercise, then the ch'i moves freely, sustaining life and strength. If we do not take care of our bodies, we get sick and the ch'i is interrupted or blocked. When there is paralysis, the ch'i is blocked. In acupuncture, the practitioner uses the principles of ch'i to open the blocked channels and direct the flow of ch'i or energy through the body.

3.1 Everything is Alive with Ch'i

Everything in your home is alive – your table, chairs, bed, stove, the art that is hanging on your wall. Everything should have a home in your house. A key holder for the keys, the books on the bookshelf. One tip is to have a "homeless box" for things that do not have a designated home, and regularly sort through it to find a permanent home.

3.2 Everything is interconnected with Ch'i

A cluttered family room, closet, home office, bedroom, or kitchen can get you stuck. You will constantly be looking for something that you lost. This then takes you into a bad mood. Your performance at home, in school, or at work suffers, or you're always late.

Another example of interconnection is when you throw a small pebble into the pond, the whole pond is affected by the rippling action of the pebble that was thrown.

3.3 Everything is changing with Ch'i

Have you heard of the saying, "The only thing constant in my life is change?" Move things around in your home and watch the positive change that follows.

3.4 Clutter

Clutter refers to any object, item, or energy that is stagnant, unnecessary, or obstructive in a given space. Clutter can negatively influence, or even completely block, the flow of ch'i and events in many areas of your life. Clutter blocks the flow of positive energy (ch'i). Clutter creates stagnation and stuckness. Clutter attracts negative energy and misfortune. Clutter affects mental clarity, focus, and productivity.

Physical clutter can mean excess belongings, mess, and disorganization.

Energetic clutter can mean negative emotions, stagnant energy, and unresolved issues.

Visual clutter can mean overwhelming colors, patterns, or decorations.

By clearing clutter, you can improve energy flow and balance, enhance mental clarity and focus, boost your mood and overall well-being, and attract positive energy and opportunities.

3.5 How can clutter affect our feng shui?

Clutter can negatively affect our Feng Shui by:

1. Blocking the flow of energy (ch'i) in our homes or dwellings.
2. Negatively impacting our mental well-being and mood.
3. Bringing negative ch'i in.
4. Damaging our surroundings.
5. Lowering air quality in the home.
6. Creating a sense of chaos.
7. Preventing positive energy from entering the home.
8. Hindering the flow of energy in certain rooms or areas of the home.

In all areas of our life, clutter should be avoided as much as possible. These are the things that we no longer need. A rule of thumb; keep only things that you love and use. If not, it's out the door or put in boxes visited every six months. If you definitely will not use them anymore, sell them, give them away, donate or throw them away. Life is too precious and short to have all this baggage that we are carrying. If you don't need it anymore, make it someone else's treasure. You will feel lighter and it will show.

3.6 Clutter in the Different Guas of your home can Symbolize Obstacles or Problems

1. Clutter in the career/ life path gua indicates a lack of progress and promotion in your career.
2. Clutter in the love and relationships gua indicates communication issues, probably keeping secrets from each other.
3. Clutter in the family/ancestors gua indicates family disagreements and wanting to break away from the family.
4. Clutter in the wealth/ prosperity/ abundance gua can make you confused and uncertain about your financial future.
5. Clutter in the center can block the ch'i from flowing to the different areas of your home.
6. Clutter in the helpful people/mentors/travel gua can prove difficulty in finding the right people. You will always be drawn to the people who will turn out to be the wrong people for you.

7. Clutter in the children and creativity/ inner growth gua can create communication problems between parents and children.
8. Clutter in the Spirituality/Knowledge/Wisdom gua can block you from learning things. Things that you try to learn get foggy and hard to grasp.
9. Clutter in the fame and reputation/ recognition gua can make it difficult for you to serve your community because of confusion and sometimes paranoia about whether people are praising you for your service or talking behind your back.

3.7 Acupuncture

Acupuncture is a medical practice that aims to restore balance to the body's ch'i. It involves inserting thin needles into specific points on the body to open the channels to stimulate the flow of ch'i. It is based on the concept of ch'i and the flow of energy in the body.

Acupuncture is believed to restore balance to the body's energy, promoting health and well-being.

Acupuncture is a holistic approach to health that aims to restore balance and promote well-being through the stimulation of specific points on the body.

Ch'i is the vital energy that flows through the body, and acupuncture is the medical practice that aims to open blocked channels of the body to restore the flow of that energy.

Both ch'i and acupuncture aim to restore balance to the body's energy. Both are based on the concept of the body's interconnectedness.

Chapter Four: The Yin and Yang Theory

The yin and yang theory describes the interconnected and interdependent nature of opposites in the universe. Yin and yang represent two complementary forces that interact and influence each other, creating a dynamic balance and harmony.

Yin is associated with receptivity, coldness, darkness, passivity. It represents the feminine, moon, night, and water. The qualities of Yin are: nurturing, intuitive, submissive, and introspective, right side of the body.

Yang is associated with creativity, warmth, light, and activity. It represents the masculine, sun, day, and fire. The qualities of Yang are: assertive, logical, dominant, and extroverted, left side of the body.

The key aspects of the Yin and Yang theory are:
1. Opposites are interconnected and inseparable.

2. Balance and harmony through the union of opposites.

This ancient philosophy offers insights into the dynamic balance and interconnectedness of all things, encouraging us to embrace and harmonize opposites in our lives.

When you are decorating your home, consider balancing the yin and yang of your area. If it is too yin, it is depressing. If it is too yang, it is overwhelming and too active. There has to be a balance between the yin and yang in your environment.

Chapter Five: The Five Element Theory

Water

Wood

Fire

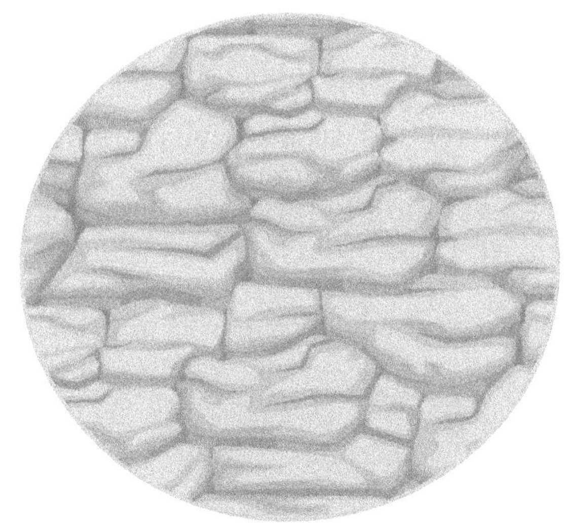

Earth

Metal

Feng Shui believes that there are five elements present in the entire universe. These are water, wood, fire, earth, and metal.

5.1 Characteristics of the five elements

<u>Water</u>

It is closely related to creativity and emotions. Water represents flow, movement, and change. Water is calming and soothing, promoting relaxation and tranquility. Water reflects images, symbolizing introspection and self-reflection. Bodies of water, sea, lake, the rain are examples of water.

Season: winter

Colors: midnight blue, black, blue-gray

Shapes: undulating, horizontal, irregular, wavy, free-form

Wood

It symbolizes health and wellness. Wood encourages being open to new ideas and opportunities. Wood promotes growth and expansion in personal and professional life. Wood can be trees, grass, or any other living plant.

Season: Spring

Colors: green

Shapes: tall, columnar, tall rectangles, tall verticals

Fire

It is associated with passion, love, and romance. Fire is considered masculine and yang in nature. Fire is associated with leadership, action, movement, and energy. Fire is also associated with anger, frustration, and aggression. Fire can be any kind of heat or light. The sun and bonfire are examples of fire.

Season: summer

Colors: red, the color of flame

Shapes: triangle, sharp points, sharp edges

Earth

It is associated with stability and permanence. Earth is associated with grounding and centering energies. Earth is associated with nourishment for oneself and others. Earth is associated with a connection to a higher power. Soil for our crops, the land where we build our houses, where we mine jewels are examples of earth.

**Season:** end of summer

**Colors:** yellow, terra cotta, brown, beige

**Shape:** Square

Metal

It is usually associated with gold or money. It can also be related to a sword or dagger. Metal is associated with organization, structure, and order. Metal represents clarity, precision, and mental focus. Metal is strong, resilient, and can withstand challenges. Metal is associated with the ability to bring order out of chaos and create a sense of calm. Jewels, gold, and natural stones are examples of metal.

**Season:** autumn

**Colors:** white, gray, metallic

**Shapes:** spherical, circular, oval, domed, and arched, representing unity and wholeness.

5.2 There is the circle of life and There is the Cycle Of Elements.

The enhancing cycle, the controlling cycle, and the weakening cycle are as follows:

5.3 The Enhancing Cycle

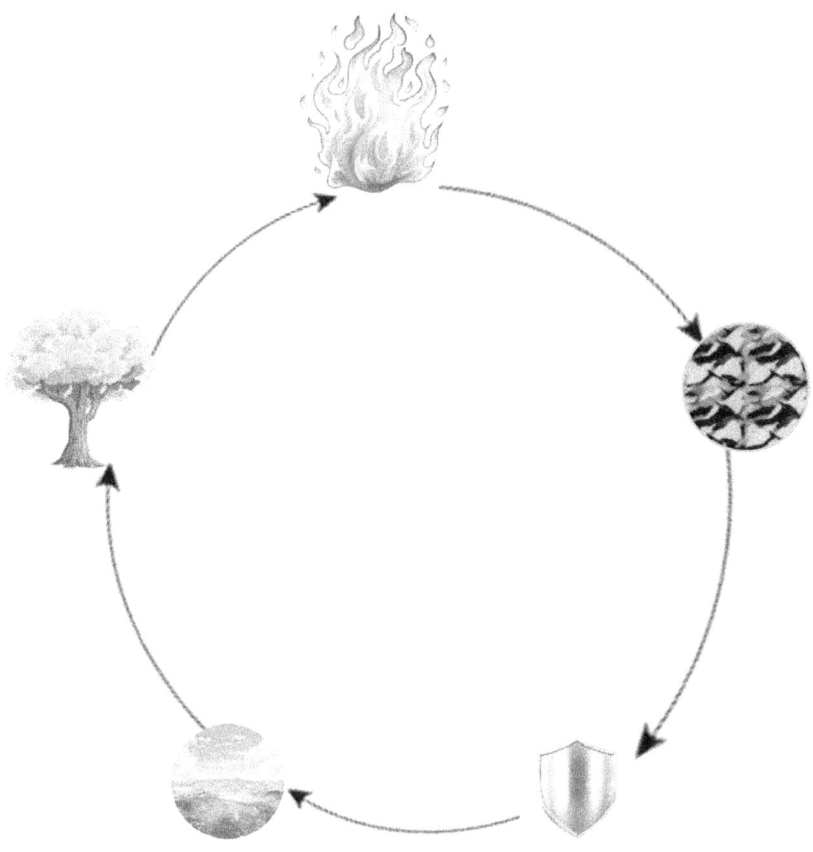

- Water nourishes wood.
- Wood fuels fire.
- Fire creates earth.
- Earth produces metal.
- Metal holds water.

5.4 The Controlling Cycle

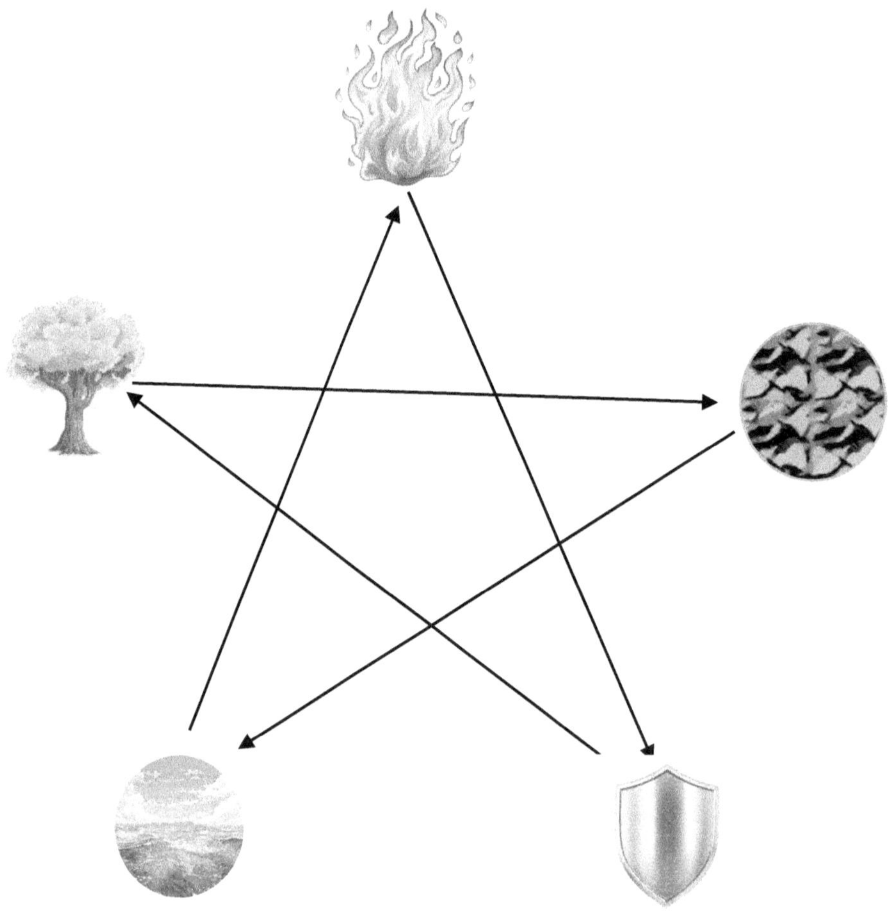

- Water extinguishes fire.
- Fire melts metal.
- Metal Chops Wood.
- Wood dominates earth.
- Earth obstructs water.

5.5 The Weakening Cycle

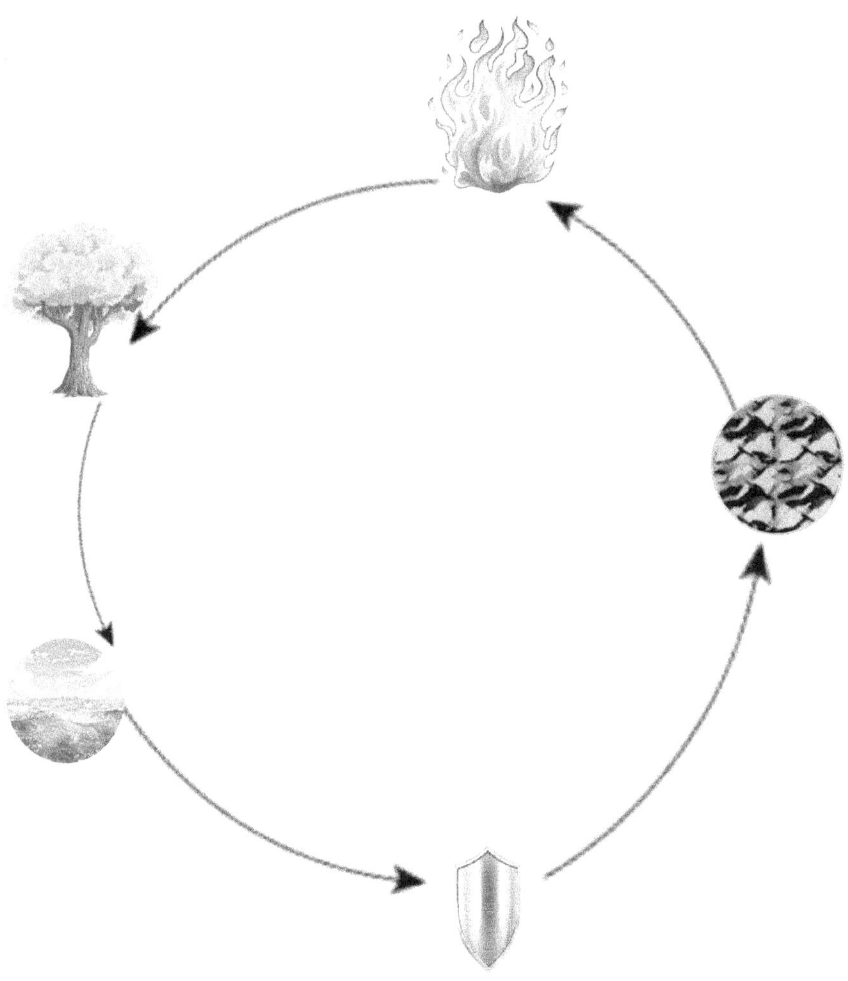

- Water corrodes metal.
- Metal reduces earth.
- Earth reduces fire.
- Fire burns wood.
- Wood draws from water.

These cycles are constantly happening, day in and day out. If we know where, how, and when to place ourselves in alignment with the right elements at the right places and periods, we become more balanced and in harmony with our environment.

These elements are constantly coming in and out of our lives. And, as one of these elements, we are constantly going in and out of other people's lives. Other people are also constantly coming in and out of our lives. Everyone is connected in one way or another ... in so many different ways!

5.6 The Bagua Map

Wealth and Prosperity	Fame and Reputation	Love, Marriage and Relationships
Family and Health	You and your well-being	Children & Creativity
Knowledge and Self Cultivation	Career	Helpful People and Travel

"Ba" means eight and "Gua" means area in Chinese. It is a Feng Shui tool which has eight sides and a center signifying the nine aspirations of life. It is a map which, when superimposed on the different areas or rooms of your home, we can assess how the ch'i, yin and yang forces and the different feng shui elements are working together in an auspicious way. We, then, can tell whether to leave them alone or rearrange, add stuff or take away stuff. The center of the map signifies "You," the most integral part of the map. The center of your home connects all the other rooms which signify the different aspirations in your life and "You" will bring them to reality. It is important, therefore, that your well-being is addressed and well taken care of.

Terah Collins, author of "Western Guide to Feng Shui," beautifully described how easily the Bagua map and what it represents is applied to our daily lives. Instead of using the compass for directions, the Bagua map is superimposed on the blueprint of the home or business using the entrance quadrant as the guideline.

5.7 Challenges and solutions in the Bagua areas

I Call These Colors of Life:

1. The bathroom with a leaking faucet. Everything in the home should be functional. Fix the leaking faucet. Replace busted light bulbs.
2. Cluttered spaces. Clear the hallways. Nothing should be behind the doors. Fix sticking doors. The hinges should be oiled and not stuck. Drawers and doors should open easily. Nothing should be cramped up in the drawers.
3. Throw away old keys that don't open any lock.
4. Donate old magazines. You can now find everything on the internet and on your phone.

5. Regularly clean out under your kitchen sink and bathroom sink.

6. Regularly clean your microwave and stove.

7. Throw away old prescriptions and over the counter medications.

8. Periodically open windows.

9. Get rid of clothes that you haven't worn in six months.

Chapter Six: The Nine Aspirations of Life

1. Career/Life Path/Life Purpose
2. Love/Marriage/Partnership/Relationships
3. Family/Ancestors/Heritage/Health
4. Wealth/Prosperity/Finances/Abundance
5. You and your well-being at the center
6. Helpful People/Mentors/Travel
7. Children/Creativity/Inner growth
8. Knowledge/Self-cultivation/Spirituality/ Wisdom/Personal growth
9. Fame and Reputation/Recognition/Community Service

Let's break down what this all means. Everyone or almost everyone would like to achieve one or all of their life's aspirations. Why not? It's free to think about it! It's free to dream! If we can think it, we can do it!

Feng Shui means wind and water. Wind is the invisible "thinking it" and water is the visible "doing it" ....making it our reality.

In every aspect of our lives, we encounter challenges, trials, speed bumps, hurdles, oppositions.

At times we become discouraged. We lose our reason — our "why."

But why? Why do we lose sight of our aspirations? Would we not want to change the situation? Don't we aspire for a better outcome? Then, let's get to work on how to make it better!

6.1 *Life's Aspirations Chart*

Life's Aspirations	Elements	Objects	No.	Colors	Shapes	Enhancing Cycle	Controlling Cycle	Location in your Home
Career/ Life path/ Life purpose	Water	Fountains, waterfalls, aquariums, birdbath, fish tanks	1	Black, blue-gray, midnight blue	Wavy, free-form, irregular, undulating	Water nourishes Wood	Earth obstructs Water	Middle front
Love/Relationships/Marriage/ partnership	Earth	Pairs of items Ex. Two red candles, pictures of lovers, symbols of love, heart	2	White, Pink, Red	Square	Earth Produces Metal	Wood diminishes and dominates Earth	Far right rear
Family/ health/ Ancestors	Wood	Family pictures, living plants, flowers	3	Green	Rectangular	Wood fuels Fire	Metal Chops Wood	Middle Left
Wealth/Prosperity/Abundance	Wood	Jade Plants, Money Tree, Lucky Bamboo	4	Green, Purple	Rectangular, Columnar, Tall	Wood fuels Fire	Metal Chops Wood	Far left rear
Well-being/ Meditation/ You	Earth	Pottery Ceramics Crystals	5	Yellow, Tan, Brown, Beige	Squares	Earth produces Metal	Wood diminishes and dominates Earth	Center
Helpful people/ Mentors/ Travel	Metal	Anything Metallic	6	White, Gray	Round, oval	Metal holds Water	Fire melts Metal	Front right
Children and Creativity/ Inner Growth	Metal	Anything Metallic	7	Pastels, White, Gray	Round, oval, spherical	Metal holds Water	Fire melts Metal	Middle right
Knowledge/ Self Cultivation/ Wisdom/ Spirituality	Earth	Pottery, terracotta, crystals	8	Brown	Squares	Earth Produces Metal	Wood diminishes and dominates Earth	Front Left
Fame & Reputation/ Recognition	Fire	Candles, Any Red in Color	9	Dark purples to bright reds	Triangular, spiky, pyramidal, cone-shaped	Fire creates Earth	Water extinguishes Fire	Middle rear

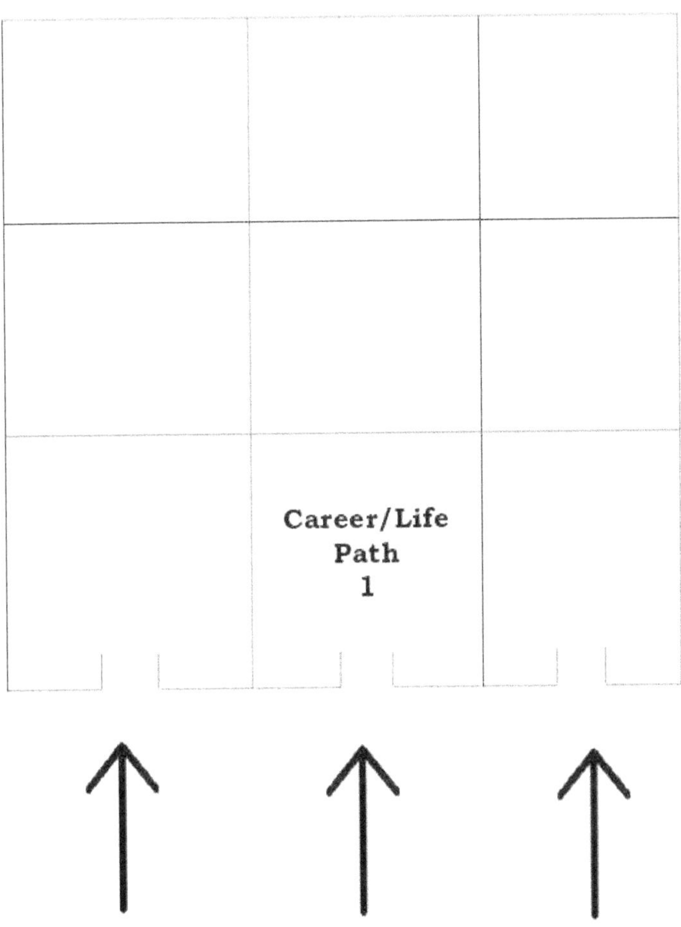

Entrance Quadrant

6.3 I am on the calendar page?

Elizabeth is a Doctor of Physical Therapy. She started her studies in the Philippines and then was offered a chance to work in the United States. Her challenge was that she had to go alone and leave her family behind. She had a hard time concentrating at work and at the same time thinking about her family that she left behind. Her mind was divided. She was alone in New York, where the agency sent her to work. She had to prove herself to her employer, that she could be an asset to the company.

After one year, she was relocated to Indiana, in an out-patient clinic. As the only Filipino in a mostly American-populated clinic, she had to prove herself again, that she could handle different cases and was able to deal with the employer and her patients.

After three years of working as a traveling Physical Therapist, she decided to work in a hospital setting. Rotating to the different hospital floors, from Intensive Care Unit to Cardiac, Orthopedics, Rehabilitation, etc., which was another challenge, but at the same time, fulfilling because she was recognized by one of her cardiac patients and was put on their calendar page. See! Patience, tenacity, hard work, compassion, and discipline will bring you to success in your chosen profession.   Aspiration + Action = Positive outcome.

6.4 *Please, Release me!*

Anna called me to help her figure out what was causing her nightmares and fears. I went to her house and saw this brown, medium-sized dog tied up by the entrance. The dog was far from the people coming to the door, but I got scared as I walked closer to the front door. A barking dog at the entrance will scare people away. I had to call Anna when I got close to the front door to come and pick me up.

There can be two meanings of this scenario. The positive meaning can be for protection. The dog symbolizes protection, loyalty and safety for the residents of the house.

The other meaning can represent obstacles in one's life, such as feeling trapped and feeling restricted and limited in some way. The dog's inability to move freely may indicate Anna's inability to move forward or lack of progress in her career.

Anna called me because she was having nightmares. With this information, I thought of the negative meaning of the nightmare. Her dog tied up by the entrance can prevent opportunities from coming in. The dog can signify the blockage.

I recommended that she move the dog to the back of the house or a designated pet area, which she did. She placed a bird bath in the front of her house to replace the dog. She also placed a colorful, welcoming mat.

Shortly after the consultation, the nightmares went away and Anna enjoyed a work promotion. Intention + Action = Positive outcome.

Life is a journey and an adventure.   Enjoy the ride!

The number one is the number of the career gua. Rightfully so! The reason the career gua is number one and located in the center front of your home is because a career/job/life purpose is important to human dignity. We are told, to grow up, to go to school, then go out there, do what you love to do, make the most of what you have, be the best you can be and claim your place in society.   Help yourself and your family while helping others. This will not happen without hard work and dedication, and purpose in life.

The career/life path gua is located in the center front of your home. The element that resides here is water. Water symbolizes knowledge, wisdom, communication   and   travel.   No   wonder "knowledge and wisdom" gua and "Helpful people and travel" gua want to stay close by. They would like to get some of what this area offers.

The career area is best activated with the water element, like a fountain, a fish tank with eight gold fish and one black fish, which is believed to protect and take any bad feng shui from everyone in that home. So, if one day, you come home to see the black fish dead, just be grateful it was the black fish and not you nor anyone in the family. Pick up the dead fish and replace it, and thank the fish for being there to take the bad feng shui.

Place a birdbath or a fountain outside your door or on the front yard to attract wild birds to bring in the good news of opportunities.

Make sure your house number is clearly visible from the street during the day and lit at night to let yourself be known.

Use a dark blue or black rug at your door to symbolically allow the opportunities to flow in like water.

The color of career gua is black, blue-gray or dark blue. Do you like black doors? Dark blue door? Blue gray? These colors activate and intensify the luck of this area.

Hang wind chimes outside your door to bring in the ch'i of opportunities or the ch'i of promotion. Make sure the front door and all your doors fully open, nothing behind the doors.

A green plant here will symbolize career growth.

You can put a turtle here to symbolize strength and endurance, and steady growth.

Be sincere! Do you want a job that most describes you? A job that you see yourself in? A job that will develop you? A job that will bring out the best in you? Then pursue it! What is your passion? Do you like helping people? Do you like taking care of endangered animals? Do you like art?

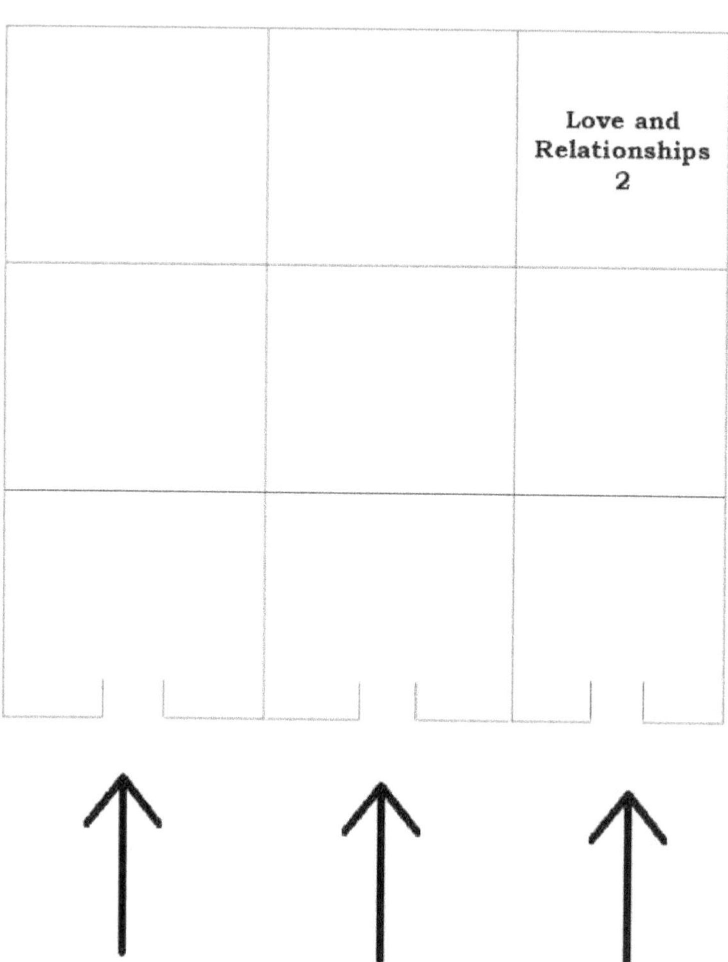

Entrance Quadrant

6.6 *Let's Talk Love*

According to Pharisiah Gail, author of "Daily Dose of Sunshine" and "Choose to Rise", Love and relationships are the tapestry of our lives, woven with threads of joy, intimacy, and connection. Yet, amidst the beauty lies a labyrinth of challenges that can strain even the strongest bonds. These challenges, if left unaddressed, can corrode the foundation of relationships, leaving behind scars of mistrust and resentment. She further talks about some problems and challenges to a meaningful relationship:

1. Communication breakdown: the silent treatment.

2. Trust issues: the shadow of doubt.
3. Balancing independence and togetherness: the dance of autonomy.
4. Conflict resolution: navigating stormy waters.
5. Emotional intimacy: nurturing the heart connection.
6. External stressors: weathering life's storms together.

How do we make it better?

1. Acknowledging and addressing the challenges of communication breakdown, cultivating the art of active listening and empathetic understanding. Setting aside ego and defensiveness, partners and friends alike can create safe spaces for open

dialogue where thoughts and feelings are expressed without fear of judgment.

2. Building trust requires patience, transparency, and a willingness to confront the underlying issues head-on. Through honest communication and consistent actions that demonstrate integrity and reliability, individuals can begin to mend the fracture of trust.

3. Finding the balance between independence and togetherness requires open communication and mutual respect for boundaries. By honoring each other's autonomy and supporting individual growth and pursuits, partners and friends can foster a sense of freedom within the confines of their relationships.

4. Effective conflict resolution requires patience, empathy, and a willingness to compromise. Active listening, empathy, and a commitment to finding common ground are essential ingredients for resolving conflicts healthily and constructively.

5. Nurturing intimacy requires vulnerability, authenticity, and a willingness to be truly seen and understood by others. Expressing gratitude, affection, and appreciation for one another can also strengthen the emotional bond between partners or friends.

6. Navigating external stressors requires teamwork, resilience, and a shared commitment to weathering life's storms together. Effective stress management

strategies, such as setting realistic goals, practicing self-care, and seeking professional help when needed, can also help individuals cope with external pressures while preserving their relationships.

Well said, Phar!

6.7 I am Woman, hear me roar!

I had a client who wanted more out of her marriage. Her complaint was, "I feel invisible in this relationship. I feel that my words don't matter, and worse, I feel that I don't have a voice in this marriage. I feel stuck and unappreciated."

She took me around her house for a tour. We ended up in her bedroom. Her bedroom bath was messy and her bathtub faucet was leaking. Her bathroom was also located in the "Love and relationships" gua of her home.

The bed spaces on each side of their queen bed were very unequal! The space on her side of the bed was almost nothing. It was almost against the wall, which explains her feeling of being stuck and having no voice. His space on his side of the bed was almost half of the bedroom space, which meant that he was dominating the relationship.

I recommended her to fix her leaking bath tub faucet and put on green and brown towels. Water is the dominant element in the bathroom. Too much water will drain your fortune and partnership away, so you want to weaken the water's dominance by putting in the wood element which is color green. Earth also controls water and the brown towel represents it. Compliment your bathroom décor with the elements fire and metal (two red candles on metal holders).

She moved her bed towards the center of the bedroom with the headboard against the wall and equal spaces on each side of the bed. After doing all this, she started seeing changes and said she felt better and felt she had more freedom to express herself. She started to feel visible and heard, and her words were appreciated more by her husband. Wow, this minor transformation fixed the problem! Let your feng shui eyes guide you to make changes to make things better. Intention + Action = Positive outcome.

6.8 Take your fake devotion with you!

Another client, Karina, called me to check her home feng shui. She wanted my feng shui eyes and a feel about her home. The entrance was colorful with different colored potted flowers. As soon as we got into the house, I saw the staircase at the center of the house. When we went upstairs, I was greeted by a beautiful vase filled with dried, spiky plants and leaves like vintage at the entrance of their bedroom.

In the bedroom, the California king bed was about three feet from the wall, and she said that was her space. The other side of the bed was about half of the huge bedroom, and this was the space of her husband.

At the bottom of the bed was a dresser with a huge mirror.

Karina was a counselor and her husband was a successful owner of five freight trucks and he drove one of his trucks.

This arrangement, according to Karina, "Is my dream marriage." She was beaming when she said, "I am very lucky to have this kind of arrangement. He leaves for about three weeks, then he comes home just in time when I would start to miss him. Then he would leave again after three weeks, just in time when we start to get into each other's nerves. At the same time, we are very financially comfortable."

We got together a few months after my consultation. She said that they divorced because her husband had been unfaithful. Oh boy!

Let's analyze Karina's home feng shui. The staircase was in the middle of the house, indicating potential health and cardiac issues. The vase outside the couple's bedroom with dried stems and leaves looking like vintage, indicating a marriage that is not nourished... fake affection. The bed space between her side and the wall is much narrower than the space of the husband's, signifying that the husband is in full control of their union. She felt stressed and unappreciated. The mirror directly at the bottom of the bed signifies multiple images of people, places, and objects that would like to be involved and included in this marriage. This is very unsettling!

Before the consultation, I asked her what she wanted to get out of this consultation and what her concerns were. She replied, "Nothing, I just wanted you to see my home feng shui in general.

The love and relationships gua of your home is located in the far right corner of your home. The dominant element of this area is Earth. Earth is stable and reliable. However, Earth can also be overbearing and unwilling to make changes. The shape of Earth is square. Love and relationship colors are the colors of Valentine's Day; red, white and pink. The number associated with this area is the number two. So, if you are looking for love, don't sleep on a twin bed. Sleep on a queen or king bed, if you have the space. Sleeping on a twin bed does not allow anyone into your life ... not even the half who will make you whole. The picture on the wall of yourself... alone, screams that you want to be alone tonight!

What if your love and relationships gua is missing? What if it is a bathroom ... with a leaking faucet? A kitchen? A hallway, a living room, a laundry room?

How do you balance this area? You can put happy pictures of you and your partner on the wall. If there is no partner yet, put pictures of a happy couple. You can also put two red candles on metal holders. You can turn on soft music that makes you in the mood for love. Now, do you feel the love? Whatever you put in this room, you have to have the right intention. Intention + Action = Positive outcome.

If the love and relationships gua is a bathroom ... with a leaking faucet, you have to fix the faucet first. Then, fix everything that is broken. Replace the busted light bulb. Unclog the clogged toilet. Put pink and red towels, put flowers or plants. Make the bathroom attractive so that you feel romantic when you go there.

If the love and relationships gua is the kitchen, red and pink aprons and kitchen towels.

If the love and relationships gua is missing, are you out of luck? No, you can use whatever space there is. If it is a deck, you can put potted plants or flowers. You can hang two heart-shaped crystals by the window wherein the different colors of the rainbow bring good and vibrant love energy. Figurine of lovers. Light the deck at night.

If you are married or in a relationship, hang happy pictures of you and your partner.

Place two red hearts in this area. This will spice up your current relationship or, if you are single, you will find a new and exciting one.

Remove anything from your bedroom that reminds you of work.

6.9 *Family/ Ancestors/ Health*

Family/
Ancestors/
Health
3

Entrance Quadrant

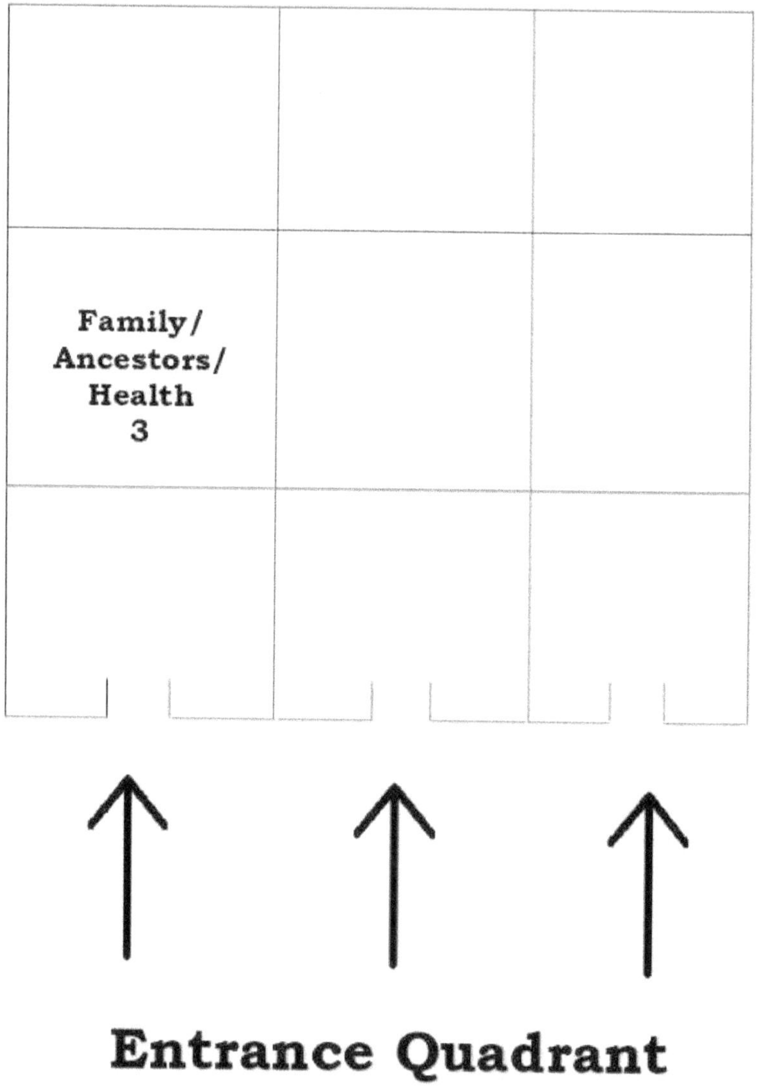

6.10 It is for your own good!

Grace is a military veteran married to another military serviceman. They have two girls. Grace said, "Growing up, my parents always showed me and my siblings how things worked in life, that we cannot always have everything we wanted. But my parents showed us unconditional love, and very important, they instilled in us the importance of education. They told us that education is our treasure that no one can take away from us. With this treasure, we can be anything we want to be and we can be the captain of our own ship, and direct our own course."

"There's also trials and tribulations. My parents both worked to help each other support me and my siblings. We are a family of two boys and five girls. My one brother passed away at an early age, which saddened my whole family, relatives, and friends. My oldest brother also took it upon himself and assumed the role of a parent when my parents were not home. He was very strict and gave us a difficult time socializing and going out with friends. We also had to hide when we went out on a date. The environment that he created made us hate and avoid him. His response to being very strict was, "This is for your own good."

The experience that I had with my brother affected how I raised my girls. Although my parents were very loving and reasonable, my oldest brother gave us a difficult time. And, sadly, that was how I raised my daughters ... very strict.

There would be arguments and confrontations almost every day when they were teenagers. This made my life miserable and I suffered from depression, anxiety, and developed chronic conditions.

"But, as their mother, and the adult in the home, I learned to compromise and control myself. I had to learn it quickly before things went out of hand. I learned to put my pride and anger aside and talked to them as calmly as I can about the importance of being able to tell me what was going on in their lives and how I can help them with their growing pains, problems and concerns.

I reassured them that I will always be there for them and I will always love them."

"I thank God for giving me the strength to make the effort, which paid off. My relationship with my husband and our daughters has become stronger than ever."

"My one daughter has a three and a half year-old Wyatt, now, who we enjoy taking care of and babysitting. My other daughter is still single and enjoying her life and career in the military."

It's amazing how loved ones can change us into better versions of ourselves."

Well said, Grace!

6.11 I am your humble princess!

Minnie, originally from India, mother of two successful daughters, said, "I had a privileged life. I was brought up like a princess. My parents were very disciplined and never showed arrogance. They were humble, religious and God-fearing.

"I was educated in the convent until high school. My maternal grandfather had a Masters in English and the school principal and my maternal grandmother was a housewife."

"I have not seen my paternal grandparents. I know, through my dad, uncles and aunts, that we have royal blood. My paternal grandfather also had a Masters in English and had his own school. Until today, he still has his statue standing in that school."

Her two daughters love and respect Minnie. She humbly concluded, "I hope I have been able to pass on at least fifty percent of what I was taught."

Minnie has raised two beautiful girls who turned out to be respectable, independent and very educated young women.

Chapter Seven: The Importance of Education and Culture

Dr. Joy said, "Due to my father's struggles, he often emphasized two things: 1. Education. 2. Culture. Because he was unable to finish his degree, it was very important that I did. He often reminded me that anything can be taken away from me, except my education and knowledge. This has been the source of motivation for me as I pursued a career working to help others."

"As a professional and a parent, I believe it is important to inspire children to be curious about the world and to be globally aware. I believe in teaching children to not only appreciate, communicate and interact with people across different cultures and in other countries, but also provide them with a stronger sense of cultural identity in an effort to preserve their own culture. When I became a parent, it was important that I share about the people, places and stories of our families being unique to who my children are. I believe that knowing about their family history and ancestors will help strengthen their connection to their culture."

The family/ancestors gua is located in the middle left area of your home. It is directly opposite the children and creativity gua. These two guas like each other, but not too much. The element that resides in the Children and Creativity gua is metal and the element that resides in the family/ancestors gua is wood. They are related just like children and parents. You have to have a creative relationship with your children. The wood in the Family gua wants the creativity of the children to grow and get well-nourished. The metal in the children and creativity gua will tolerate the parents for a while until they get tired and bored from the lectures and teachings of the parents and they become hostile and impatient with the parents, just like the axe in the metal chopping the wood in the family/ancestors gua. To activate the family/ancestors gua, put healthy, hardy plants. This will be harder for the axe of the children and creativity gua when they decide to strike.

Your exercise equipment is good in this area as it will help you to remember to exercise and be healthy.

A turtle is also a good animal to put in this area as it signifies strength and hardiness and long life. Just like the turtle, your family will have your back.

Hanging family pictures, framed in wood, in this area, will help togetherness and foster closer relationships.

You can also display family heirlooms or antiques that you love.

7.1 *Wealth/ Prosperity/ Abundance/ Finances*

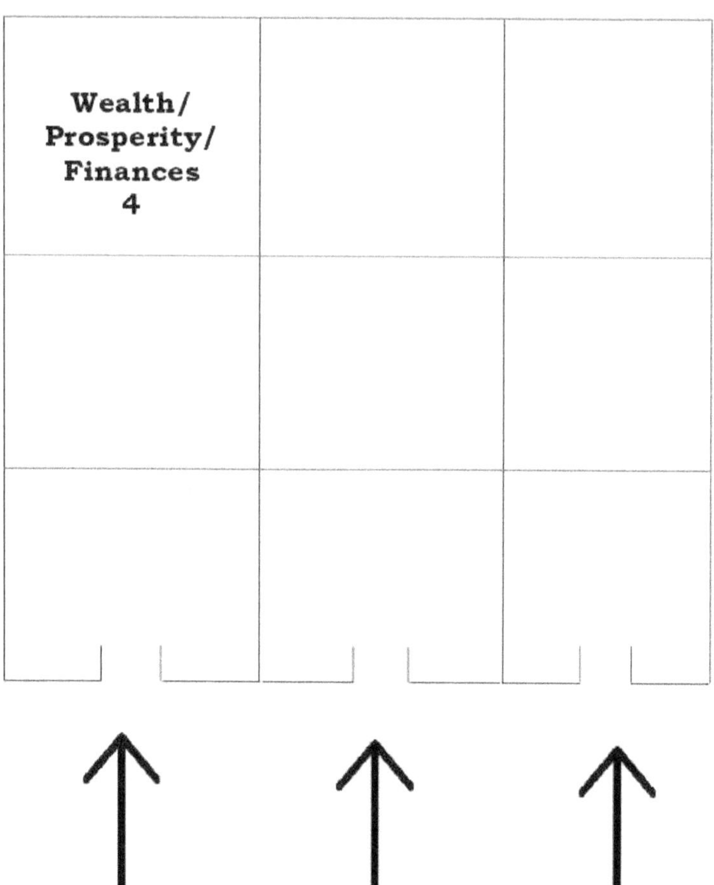

7.2 I am Enjoying My House by the Ocean

Mina, a retired registered nurse, knows a thing or two about creating wealth and prosperity. She said that there were a lot of challenges in wealth-creation and building at the very start. "It takes a job and investing to make money. And then, we had the boys. Spending time with them and enjoying them, although we loved it, took us away from looking for investment opportunities. More challenges came with raising and watching them grow."

"As the boys started to be more independent and self-sufficient, and with the help and guidance of my parents, me and my husband found more time to look into investing. Between me working as a full-time registered nurse and my husband as a general contractor, together, with the help of experts and other professionals and mentors, we built and are still building a comfortable life that allows us to be more flexible with our time. Do we walk at the beach this morning, or hop on a plane to travel somewhere we haven't been to?"

"With fortune and blessings from the universe, I have more time to volunteer at my church. I give my time and service any way I can. I also help my son by helping babysit my two grandsons."

Summing it up, Mina said, "When we aspire and we work hard towards it, it will happen." Intention + Action = Positive outcome.

The wealth and prosperity gua is located at the far left rear corner of your home. Can you see what's there? Do you see and feel some wealth and prosperity? No? Because the trees outside this gua are overgrown! Your wealth is buried deep in the forest that you have created! Once you thin out those trees and dead leaves and branches, wait a week. You will find something. Intention + Action = Positive outcome.

The element that resides in this gua is wood. The color of wood is green. The shapes of wood are rectangular and vertical.   Wood represents growth.   Live plants, fresh flowers, and green objects represent the wood element. So, if you mistakenly placed the green Buddha in that area because you had no other place to put it, leave it there. See, you intuitively put it there! Just dust it every now and then. You will see the wealth and prosperity clearer.

How do we activate this area? Water feeds and nurtures wood. You can put an aquarium in this area. With the black fish? Yes, include the black fish with the eight gold fish. Let them play and swim together. That is good feng shui.

What don't we put there? Metal (axe) chops wood. Metal is a kill-joy and a party-pooper to wood. Little bits of silver charm or metal edges of the aquarium are acceptable. Water weakens metal and strengthens wood.   They also accentuate your décor, so don't worry about it. You still brought in a play of the elements, as long as the metal is not in abundance and not overwhelming.

Jade plants or the money tree are good in this area. Also, the fortune plant.

Water features like fountains will keep abundance flowing.

7.3 *You and Your Well-being*

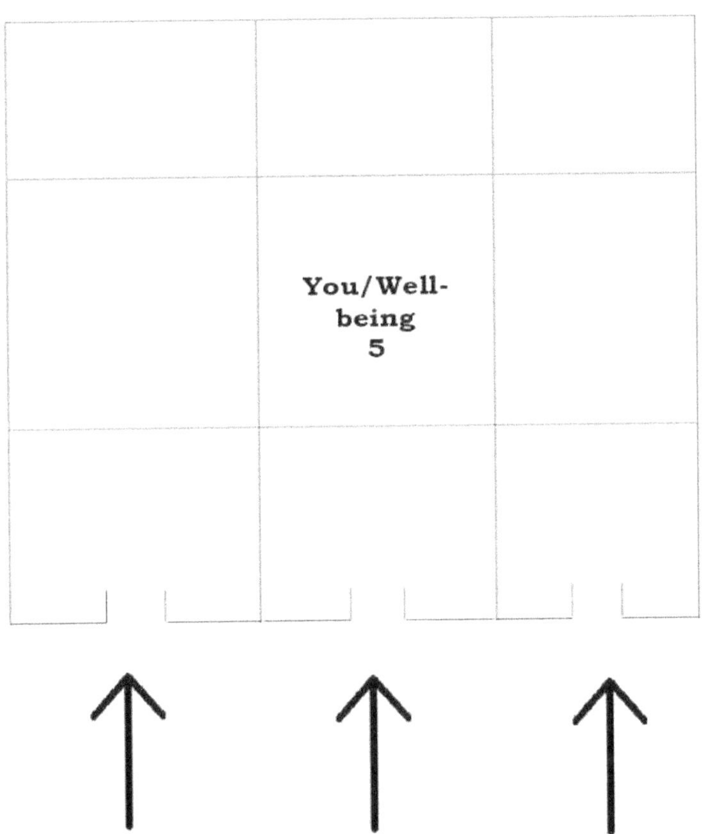

Entrance Quadrant

7.4 Meditation Leads to Flexibility

The center of your home signifies you. You are the most integral part of your home because you are the one to bring all your aspirations to fruition.

I met my yoga teacher, Chloe, through my chiropractor, who I've been seeing for over twenty years. I visit my chiropractor every six months or so, to align my aging body.

One day, while I was waiting in the reception area of the clinic, for Dr. Lochridge to see me, I saw a flyer of Hatha Yoga by Chloe. I've been curious about hatha yoga for a long time and tried to go several times, but was unable to let myself go and try it. This time, I told myself to just do it! I'm glad I did! Chloe is helping me be more flexible ... in body, mind, and spirit. I was also able to gently push my husband into her yoga class. As we get older, we are not as flexible. Hatha yoga is the gentlest stretching exercise that I have ever experienced. I did attend yoga classes offered by the gym which I was a member of when I was younger. It was much harder on my body than Chloe's class. As Chloe says at the beginning of each class, "We are just practicing. We are not in competition. Not even with ourselves."

I look up to Chloe! I think she is a very strong woman... in body, mind, and spirit. She is direct, spontaneous, and always sincere.

Chloe told me that she was beaten as a little girl, by her father, who was a Major in the Marine

Corps, stationed in Germany, during World War Two (WWll). She said that her father saw way more than a decent person should ever have to see. He came home with a severe case of post-traumatic stress disorder (PTSD), but they did not know it back then. They called it "shell shock."

One time, they were sitting around, singing, harmonizing – they had their part, and her dad was playing the ukulele. "All of a sudden, he just snaps! He started punching, kicking, and throwing us, and we would do whatever we could not to hit the corner of the piano. His hands were huge! I've been thrown from the dining room to the living room." She said that they couldn't go to the doctor because they couldn't let the doctor see how many times her ribs had been broken.

When she was old enough to think, she thought she would try to be perfect. She said, "I must be bad. That's why he's beating me. I tried to be perfect, but he kept beating me! So, when I was fourteen, I ran away from home. They put me with the big girls, and I started thinking, "Oh, you think I'm bad, I'll show you bad!" "I've spent twenty-five years being a very naughty girl."

Did she know she was going to be a yoga instructor? "No, I didn't! I was having a conversation with myself when I took the wilderness survival course. If you can do this, you can do anything! My first self-asked, "What do you want to do?" My second self   said, "I want to be a yoga teacher!" My first self said, "Why did you wait so late to tell me?" I was fifty-six! I went to yoga teacher school. I took everything and I can teach teachers at this point. So what! The real thing is that I'm here to love and serve my fellowmen and I didn't know that I hated myself. I thought that I was mad at everybody else! I used anger to scare people away from me. I used anger for everything! Then, I found out that it's a character defect, and I had to let go of it."

"I had a sponsor named Betty, and she was good at helping me. She's very gentle. I used to meditate for hours. My sponsor told me that I had to stop because I was going too far out. She asked, "How long have you been leaving your body?" Now, I can't meditate for hours. I have to stop after one hour.

"I've been meditating all this time because my mother meditated. My mother was a Christian Mystic."

"I taught meditation at Fellowship Men's Recovery for twenty-five years."

"Well-being is all one thing ... body, mind and spirit. Yoga is a doorway to the temple of the living spirit. Body, mind and spirit. If the body is not well, nothing is."

"Yoga is one of the ways I spread love. We come here and we let go ... let go of the earthly, negative energy and we are automatically filled with energy from the Great Spirit. That's why, when the class is over, we feel so different!"

Chloe is a great person! One lesson that I learned from talking to her is – do not let your past define your present and your future. Everyone can be the best they can be. You just have to allow the universe to come in and work with you. Have faith in your abilities and always pray for guidance from the Divine Power. You are worth it!

The center of your home is like the "nut" that holds all the other parts of the home together. You are that "nut." Let the "nut" be guided by the Higher Power. Ask and you shall receive. You don't have to do it alone. Father Ben, one of the priests in my parish church, said it best when he said to make Christ the nut to help you keep everything centered. Keep him at the center of your life.

Father Azam told me that he never, ever thought that he was going to be a priest. What made him? He had a self-revelation! He talked to God at a time when he had doubts and confusion about his Catholic upbringing. During the discernment week, when it was him and God – away from the distractions that cluttered his mind – "Speak to me, Lord. Lead me the way. You are my shepherd!"

The center of your home is where you go to meditate on finding your inner self and well-being … body, mind and spirit. Add a calming element, like a small water fountain or a peaceful statue.

The element that resides in this area is the earth element. To enhance the power of this gua, put objects that help you be grounded, like a bonsai plant planted in a terra cotta planter. You can also put rocks around the plant.

Activate this area if you are feeling confused and uncertain, lack clarity or direction, have emotional imbalance, have physical health issues, have stagnant energy, or have relationship problems.

Have a conversation with your Higher Power. Ask yourself what it is that you want in life. What are your dreams? What is your intention? Pay attention to what you hear. That might be the answer you are looking for. You are the most important being. Keep your eyes on the prize ... which is you!

Place a meditation carpet, a chair, soft, soothing music, and aroma therapy, and find your inner self and spirituality.

Forgive people who have wronged you and ask for forgiveness from people who you have wronged. Life is a journey. Make it beautiful! Make it in such a way that brings you closer to yourself. Love yourself! That is the only way you can love others. Allow God into your life and let Him be the light that guides you along the way.

Yellow, beige, or brown are balancing colors for this area. The center gua is the heart and nut of your home, and balancing it can have a positive impact on your overall well-being.

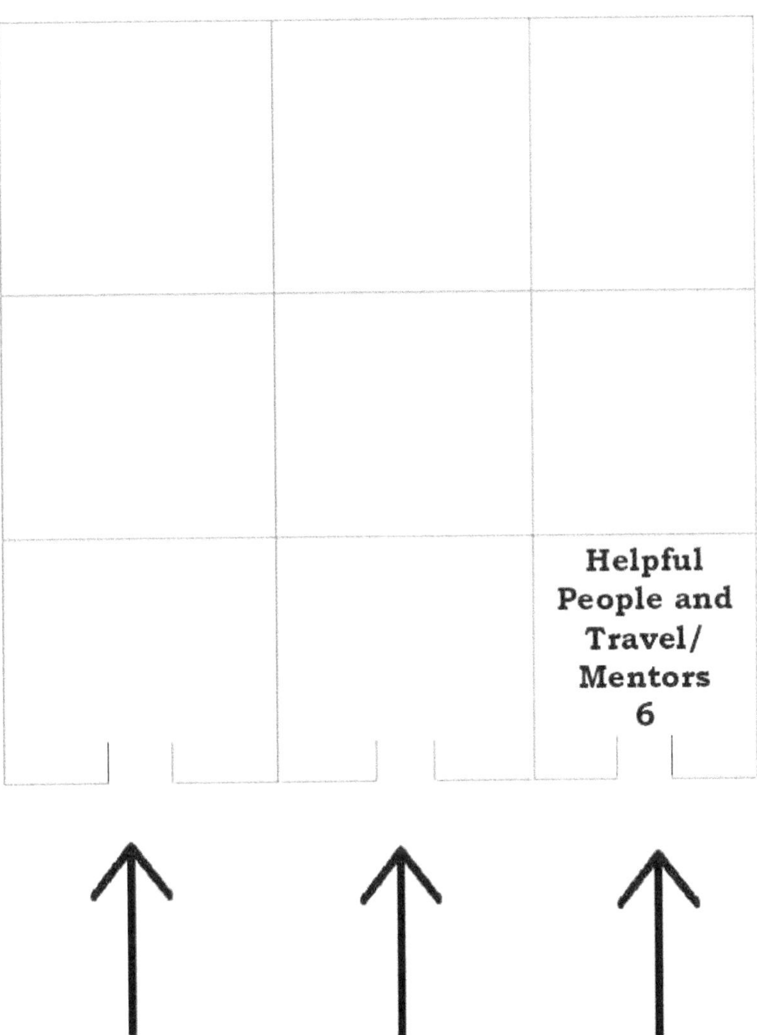

Entrance Quadrant

7.6 *Show me the Way*

Elizabeth, Doctor of Physical Therapy, said that she had mentors when she started her job here in the United States, and "I owe them a lot of gratitude." She also had helpful people who she met along the way, not necessarily her colleagues, who helped her in so many ways, when she first started especially because she was by herself in this country. Most important of all is that she always went to her Higher Power for guidance, wisdom and strength.

The Helpful People and Travel gua is located in the front right area of your home. Since it is in the entrance quadrant, the main door of your home can also be located in this area.

The Helpful People gua is responsible for attracting supportive relationships and opportunities into your life. By activating this area, you can enhance your connections with others, find helpful mentors and guides, and create a supportive environment that fosters growth and development.

Activate this gua when you feel lack of support from others, difficulty finding helpful people, feeling isolated and alone.

The element that resides in this gua is metal. Place a metal object, like a wind chime or a metal statue. Since Earth strengthens metal, you can also put a stone statue here. You can also display a cross, picture or statue of Jesus or angels. All these signify helpful people and will help bring blessings and fortune to your doorstep. Intention + Action = Positive outcome.

Pictures of airplanes or cars can enhance your travel prospects or plans.

The colors gray, white or gold activate this area.

7.7 Spiky Succulents Turned Into Helpful Succulents

Ella called me because her son was on drugs, and she was having problems with her marriage. She wanted me to see what she could do with her house feng shui to help her with these challenges.

As soon as I pulled up in front of her house, I saw potted spiky succulents in front of the main entrance, and looking around, I saw more spiky succulents on the front right corner of her yard planted on the soil.

She invited me inside her home and I saw the stairs right in the middle of the house. To the far left rear is the kitchen, to the left front is the dining area, to the far right rear is the family room and to the right front is the living room.

I also noticed that the front door is directly aligned to the back window, so I saw the back yard view from the front door.

The spiky succulents are good in the rear middle section of the home. You can put them inside, and you can put them outside, as well. It signifies fire which, when activated in this area, helps with your reputation and recognition for the service that you do to give back to your community.

The spiky succulents in the front signify hostility and it's not friendly. That probably explains the problem in the marriage and the son addicted to drugs. The front door directly aligned to the back window signifies financial instability. This means money going straight out as soon as it comes in. I would even think not enough is coming in because of the hostile entry way.

The spiky succulents in the front right of her yard do not welcome helpful people into her life. Instead, she is preventing them from coming in and helping in any way they can.

The stairs in the middle of the house signifies imbalance and can interrupt the harmonious flow of ch'i.

I asked her if she liked her succulents. She said that they were economical; they hardly needed watering and she didn't need to care for them as much. I suggested replacing the spiky succulents with rounded, friendly leaves and with colorful flowers.

I suggested putting a potted plant or a room divider between the main entrance and the back window. We would like the ch'i to meander around the house, instead of going straight out the window.

I also suggested having a nice yellow carpet and a small potted plant at the landing of her stairs.

She can add aroma therapy and soft music in that area, as well.

The center of the house is the meditation and the "You" area. This area needs to be taken care of because this is the "nut" that holds all the areas of the home together.

Even before I left, Ella was already beaming with excitement and cannot wait to make the changes.

She called me back to her house after one month to show me the changes that she made. First, she replaced the spiky succulents in her entrance with beautiful in-season-colored flowers. She replaced the spiky succulents with rounded succulents in the Helpful People area of her yard. She placed a beautiful lightweight room divider between the living room and the family room, covering the view of the back yard when you came into the house. I thought this was a creative move!

She took my suggestion and put a soft, plush yellow carpet on the stairs landing and put a little bonsai tree planted in a terra cotta planter. She was also burning aromatic incense when I came to visit.

She reported to me that she contacted people to help with her son's addiction, and she felt that her son was open to the help that would be coming his way. Her son made friends with people on the program.

She made herself more aware of finances coming in and going out by writing down the incoming finances and the expenses, and she admitted that she should have done this sooner. She confided that her husband liked the overall change, and he particularly liked the arrangement at the landing of the stairs. She was happy about the progress that was made by the simple change that she had made.

I like consultations like this!

7.8 Children and Creativity/ Inner growth

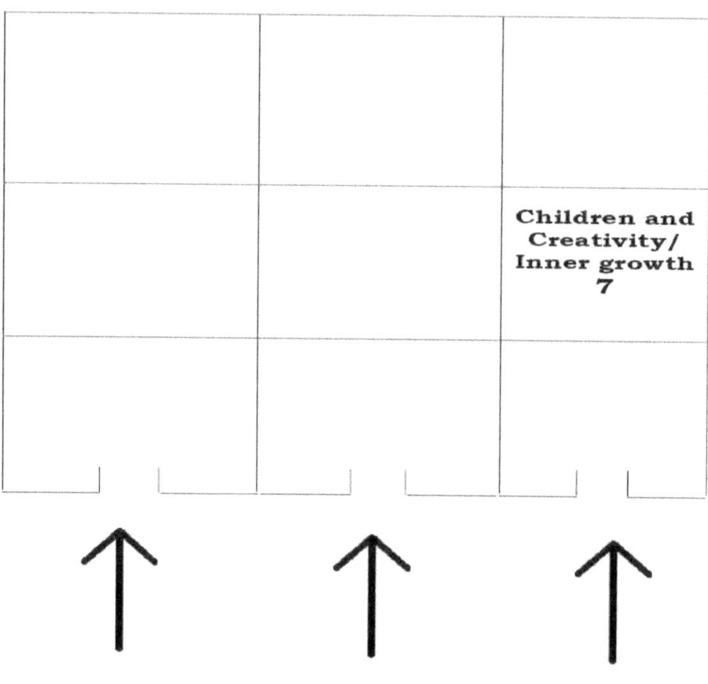

The Children and Creativity gua is located in the middle right area of your home (as you are facing the entrance quadrant of your home). It is on the right side of the center of your home. There's a reason it is located there. Parents need the help of the center to help them be centered on their beliefs and convictions and give them the strength to foster their children's curiosity and creativity. Parents need to take care of their own well-being to stay true to themselves and that is what they teach their children.

The children and creativity gua is also above the helpful people and travel. You need all the helpful people in your life to help with raising your children while remaining sane.

7.9 Sail Away, but don't forget Your Compass and Your Chart!

Bianca, who works in the military, and a mother of two young children, said that the challenge of raising young children and working hard to support them is that "I am still required to be creative and be like a child like them, and still be available to them." The challenge of raising children is that you would like your children to grow up discovering their creativity, but also worry about their safety. Parenting also means that one has to reconcile between raising children and your relationship with your husband. There should be a balance. She put it so well when she said, "Sometimes, as a parent, it seems like directing my children to research the areas in life that they are curious about and developing their interests is as risky and unpredictable as setting sail on an ocean without a compass and a chart."

7.10 Knowing who you are and Nourishing It is Big!

Another mother of two young boys, Raelyn, said that as a child, she had a lot of energy and she was always looking for ways to expend that energy. She was put into sports, piano, and singing lessons. "I needed more creative outlets. Sports was not really doing it. It got my physical energy out, but I felt I had a lot more mental energy than physical. So, I struggled to find different outlets."

"I always had the feeling of wanting to create something, to give back, but then it got to a point, at an early age, where I felt I was annoying. So, it kind of dumped into my personality. As I got older, I realized that I like singing, music. Those were the main ways I could build my character and be creative. And then, writing came into play. I like writing, making poems."

"There was a lot of mental anguish that music helped with, like going through the teenage phase of it. I remember just lying on the floor, just blasting my boom box. That made me calm."

"Having two kids, it makes it hard to be creative, but this brings everybody together. Abram likes to build tracks and legos. At times, when he is playing and I'm taking care of Micah, and he wants to play with me, I used to say, 'No, not right now." But now, I make the time because of how important it is for that creative outlet for him. I'm thankful to Peter, my husband, because he makes time and allows Abram to be creative and silly, at the same time, when he is building."

"When I started going to high school, and then meeting boys, that blocked my creative flow. I became boy-crazy instead of nourishing my inner creativity, and letting that play out. But I would always go back to singing."

"I noticed that when I stopped singing a few months ago, I started having vagal nerve problems. When I looked at what are ways to cure your vagal nerve, it said humming and singing. So now, I try to sing every day with the kids. It's funny how your body would tell you to do certain things without you realizing it is actually good for your body and mental health. A lot of it is just listening to your body and letting your body take over. If you are doing what you want to do instead of what people are telling you what to do, that will keep you young and healthy because you're being true to yourself."

"But we get caught up in distractions, like thinking that we don't have it in us. You see on social media someone drawing well, and you say to yourself, "Oh, she draws so well. I wish I could do that." You can! You just have to start. Some people have a natural ability for creativity and some people will have to work at it. But it doesn't mean that you shouldn't. It just means that maybe you have other untapped creativity that you need to learn about yourself. I think it's just knowing who you are and nourishing that. I think that's a big thing!"

7.11 Being a Parent is My Greatest Adventure

Dr. Joy continued, "Personally, becoming a parent continues to be one of my greatest adventures. The lessons they have taught me are far greater and more valuable than I ever expected."

"The attachment patterns we experience as children impact us in powerful ways throughout our lives. Understanding my attachment to my parents has provided incredible insight into making sense of my narrative and the attachment patterns I pass on to my children. Every day is a chance to learn and what we learn becomes a part of who we are."

"My children have inspired me to be flexible and not limit myself to setting rules and guidelines, be spontaneous and be more open-minded."

7.12 I Want a Mini Me!

I met a successful businessman who wanted to have children. He and his wife, an accountant, had done every fun thing under the sun that could be done. Now, they would like to settle down and have children. They both invited me to their home to see what is preventing them from having children.

I checked all the Bagua areas, and my "feng shui eyes and feel" saw the problem as clear as a sunny day. The living room is located in the Children and creativity gua and there it was – a beautiful stone fireplace. I asked if they use the fireplace. They said they did. I suggested to them to cover the fireplace with brown cloth and in front of it put a canvass on a stand and beside it, place a ceramic cup with pastel paint brushes.

Within six months, the wife was pregnant.

For someone who practices feng shui, this is an easy fix.

That is what this book is all about … to give everyone the knowledge to create their own "feng shui eyes and feel." It might be confusing in the beginning. If you just continue learning about it, it will make it easier and then you will wonder why you haven't done it sooner.

The element that resides in the Children and creativity gua is metal. Metal is the element of business and financial success. It represents clear thinking, and an upright, moral outlook. So, raising children is a serious business! You have to take care of them, nourish them, foster their curiosity and be a role model who they can base their lives on while maintaining their individuality.

Metal, with all its good qualities of clear thinking and focus, comes its negative qualities. Metal, like a knife or sword, can be violent. This can be expressed through emotional outbursts and lack of focus. Your toddler can throw tantrums when tired and sleepy. You should be able to navigate and guide and distract your mind to a better place and thinking. Taking a break and allowing your toddler to express him/herself will be the best way. When the tantrum passes, your toddler will be as good as new.

Pastel colors are good in this gua to bring out the creativity of your toddler as well as your creativity. Take a blank canvass, give your toddler pastel colored paint and brushes, and watch what he/she does with them. You might create a great, artistic child or an artistic painter. Watch what happens!

Silver and gold jewelry are also objects to house in this gua. These enhance the power of this gua to attract financial success.

Earth creates metal. Earth is the parent that nourishes metal. You can hang a crystal by the window, which enhances the power of metal. You can use terra cotta pots or bowls as your toddler's paint brush containers.

What should you not put in this area? Fire melts metal. You do not want candles and matches in this room. You do not want your precious toddler playing with fire. You do not want your precious investment going up in flames.

This area is also a good place for hobbies, crafts and artwork, card games with family and friends. This area brings out people's creative side.

Place a musical instrument, like a drum set, a piano, or a guitar, to enhance creativity.

This is a good place to hang or display children's pictures. This is also a good children's bedroom.

If you do not have a child and plan on having one, place the baby's stuff in this room.

Some pet owners treat their pets like their children, so this room can be the pet room.

Entrance Quadrant

7.14 Talking Religious and Spiritual with Father Azam

My favorite parish priest, Father Azam, was very kind to sit down with me to share his journey through the religious life. He said that he grew up in a Catholic family with very pious and religious parents. He said, "My growing up was a joyful experience. I appreciated every moment of it. Looking back and looking at my family, I can only say, Thank you, Lord."

But he said that he never, ever thought of becoming a priest. He always wanted to be either a pharmacist or a medical doctor. His father was a pharmacist and they had their own chemist shop. "And I already had two girlfriends. One was a Hindu and the other one was a Muslim and I wanted to marry both of them." I think the reason Father Azam became a priest was because he couldn't make up his mind between the two girlfriends. Bless me, Father. I'm just kidding! Father Azam is from Karachi, Pakistan. Every year, the arch diocese of Karachi organizes a vocational kind of discernment week called "Come and see." The Parish Pastor asked him if he would like to go and attend. It was the holiday season and he had no school, so he agreed to go. The discernment week was at the Monastery of Angels, where the nuns live. They spend their days and nights praying and adoring the Lord. They are cloistered nuns. This is a special calling. Although he grew up in a Catholic family, he did not like the Catholic practices. He had a passive resistance to his faith. He had doubts about the

Eucharist. He also had a difficult time with his relationship with the Blessed Virgin Mary.

His parish Pastor asked him to go to the five-day discernment "Come and See" week. This was a Eucharist adoration organized by the diocese of Karachi, Pakistan, where he is from. He was curious about this event and went. While there, he asked, "Speak to me, Lord." He felt the call when he was in that monastery for five days. He realized that he was missing something in his life. He was missing God. He said he ended up in the seminary after those five days. What a revelation! But there were challenges at the beginning of his journey to the priesthood. His biggest challenge was the English language. Although they were taught English in school, they still spoke Punjabi, their mother tongue, or Urdu, the national language of Pakistan, at home.

Another challenge for him was the culture of the different places that he moved to carry out his missionary work. He has been to Rome, Australia, Sri Lanka, France, the Philippines, and now, the United States. "In all these countries, in all my years of priesthood, one thing I can always say is Jesus is with me. He is journeying with me. He wants to encounter us. He wants to journey with us."

Three important religious figures encouraged him and served as his mentors. First was Francis Nadeem, who was a seminarian at time. He encouraged him to be a priest. During his formative years, he was guided by Father Augustine Suarez, his rector for nine years, and

Father Robert Silva, his spiritual director. These three important people in his life "helped me encounter Christ throughout my formation. And the Blessed Virgin Mary was always there."

I asked him when and how he knew that religious life was for him. He answered, "I'm still discovering. It cannot be certain because our God is a god of adventure. He leads us. He guides us. Am I certain about my vocation? I do know that God has a plan for me. But what plan He has for me? I don't know. I'm not interested in knowing because God is my Shepherd. He leads me where He wants me, not where I want. He leads me to the green pastures."

He further said that "religious life is like a family on earth and it is a wonderful family. We come from different parts of the world and with different mentalities, but with a single intention—to proclaim the Kingdom of God – to follow Jesus! That's the only aim that I have as a religious. In the end, we are human beings. God chooses us. God doesn't call the saints. God calls the sinners."

"In a mission, there are always challenges, but these challenges remind us that we have to carry on with the mission."

"Don't be afraid to encounter Jesus." That's the only message I want to tell the young people. Allow Jesus to encounter you. Allow Jesus to walk with you."

"The gift that was bestowed in me is a gift from God."

He shared the code of one of the passages by St. Eudes: "We are the missionaries of mercy sent by the Father of mercy to produce the food of mercy to offer to the merciful Father." "And that's our call."

He concluded by saying, "We are the missionaries of mercy. Jesus is with me on my journey. Jesus is there to encounter us. Let's not be afraid to encounter Him." Very profound words!

I am grateful to Father Azam for taking the time to talk to me amidst his busy schedule.

Chapter Eight: What is your why?

Chrislei practices yoga regularly, and she said that a firm mindset and purpose are necessary for self-cultivation. "You have to know the reason why you do what you do and what result you wish to get out of it."

She further said that knowledge is necessary for human existence. "Without knowledge, we cannot experience living life to its fullest. There are a lot of sources of knowledge out there, you just have to be mindful of where to get them and what kind of result you want out of that knowledge. The right knowledge can be a tool for a better life. The wrong knowledge and utilization can bring destruction to you and your loved ones."

Finally, she said that "spirituality is a consciousness of everything that surrounds us. It is the belief and awareness that you are only a part of a large universe that is shared by everyone and everything and that there is a Higher Being who we answer to and who we bring our concerns, problems, even our secrets. The Higher Being is believed to be the caretaker of this universe which we are a part of."

8.1 Divine intervention!

When me and my husband were dating, I assumed that my now husband was a Catholic like me. When he revealed to me that he was not, it was too late to back out because he had already captured my heart. But I requested that we raise our future children in the Catholic faith, to which he agreed.

We later married in the justice of peace, raised our children in the Catholic faith and later sent them to Catholic school. Then, we moved to St. Patrick's parish. We religiously went to mass every Sunday and he would go to the front with arms crossed over his chest to accept the blessing instead of the host.

During the time that we were attending masses at St. Patrick's, they picked my whole family to represent our parish for the Chrism Mass.

After that experience, my husband was so enlightened and inspired that he wanted to be a part of that religious family. He converted to the Catholic faith shortly after that experience.

I call this Divine Intervention! I thank God for these blessings! After ten years, we got married again. This time, it was at St. Patrick's church, to bless our marriage and our family.

The Knowledge/Self cultivation/Wisdom/Spirituality gua is located in the front left area of your home. In some houses, this is where the main entrance is located. So, when you enter your home, you are right there.

Like the love and relationships area, the element that resides in this gua is Earth. Unlike the Love and Relationships area, we don't put Valentine colors in this area. The colors of this area are brown and earth tones, just like the stable and mighty mountains. This is the area that helps us intellectually and gain wisdom while remaining grounded. It would be beneficial to put a sitting area in this corner and a bookshelf with books that you are interested in. Lighting up this area is helpful and it enhances your interest in reading and learning about things that you are curious about or what you are thinking about for your next business gig or money-making idea. The wisdom gua and the relationships gua are diagonally opposite each other and the element that dominates these areas is Earth. It is beneficial to have a working relationship with the ones that you love because they can show you a thing or two in the intelligence department. Working together is the key to success.

What room is your spiritual gua in? Is the bathroom there? Water signifies wealth, but if it's in the wrong gua, it can hamper or drown your spirituality and self-knowledge, thus preventing you from moving forward in life and accumulating wealth. Water in the knowledge area flushes your ability to do so. In Feng Shui, some cures mitigate these kinds of imperfections. You can move your bathroom. That would be a major and a big decision. The easier way is to put things that would control too much water by putting in place the color yellow, which is the color of Earth. Earth obstructs water. The element earth also governs this area. Brown or earth tone towels in the bathroom will definitely help.

Pictures of a mountain or a globe are best suited in this corner of your home. This signifies a vast or massive appetite for knowledge of different stuff.

Activate your knowledge/ spiritual gua when you have limited spiritual growth or connection, when you lack inspiration or motivation, or when you have strained relationships with teachers or mentors.

The knowledge/ spiritual gua is responsible for nurturing spiritual growth, inspiration and knowledge. When you activate this area, you can enhance your mental clarity, improve relationships with mentors or teachers, and create a supportive environment that fosters spiritual development and connection.

8.2 *Fame and Reputation/ Recognition*

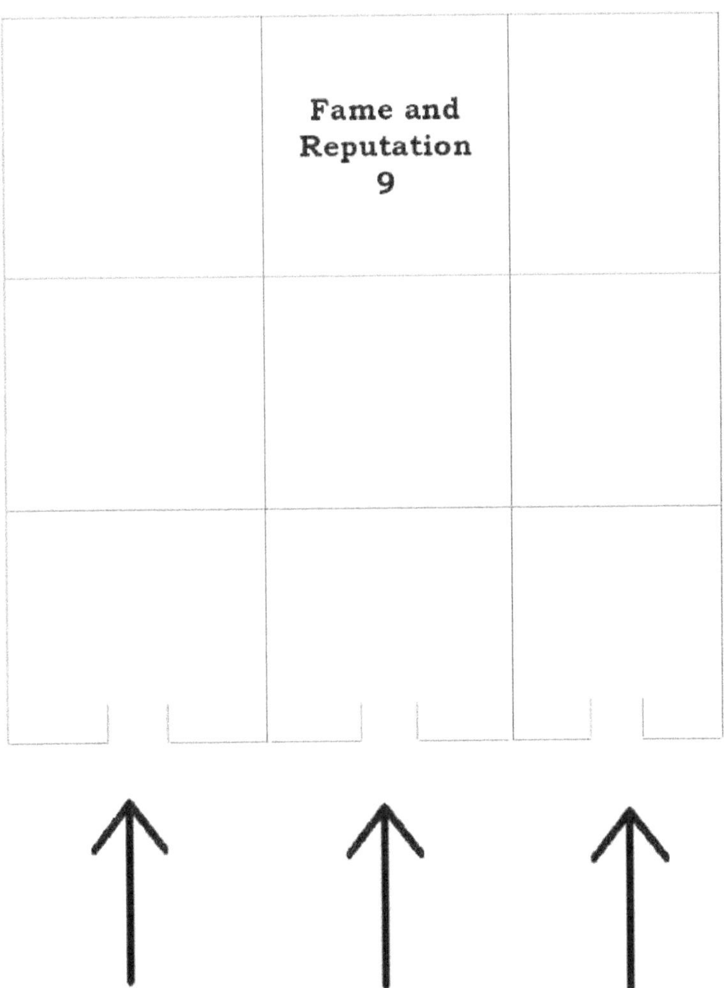

Entrance Quadrant

8.3 *Let me be the one!*

Virginia, a Marriage, Family and Child Counselor (MFCC), said that at an early age, she wanted to be a pediatrician. "When I was ten, I saw a movie about a little boy who died of leukemia. I said to myself, I wanted to be the doctor who could cure him. Throughout high school and before college, I had it in my head that I was going to become a doctor. So, when I went to the university we had already moved from Chicago to California. I went to the University of California, Riverside (UCR) because they had a program where you go straight from undergrad to medical school called the BioMed program."

"By the time I got to sophomore year, I couldn't deal with Chemistry and the hard sciences. It was such a competitive, cut-throat program, so I ended up going to Psychology and Biology – Psychobiology. Then, I found Psychology and Human Development in undergrad. I still wanted to work with kids – I wanted to work in child abuse. Then, I needed a degree in Marriage, Family and Child Counselor (MFCC). That was the licensure."

The reason I wanted to go to medicine was because my mom was a nurse. Her whole career was a registered nurse. Her good friend, Uncle Jim, was a nuclear physicist at the hospital where my mom worked. He encouraged me to be a doctor. Even for my graduation from eighth grade, he bought me a whole camera kit because he knew I liked photography.   He was encouraging and supportive of my desire to be a doctor."

There was another one, a nun. Her name was Sister Roman. I remember her telling me, and I stuck with it, and I tell my clients this, too, now. The friends that you're going to make and keep are the friends you're going to make in college. She is right! I still have a small circle of college friends." I met more people and supervisors who were my mentors. Now, I get to be a mentor to young and upcoming therapists. I end up mentoring some of the staff, as well. I get to pass on what the other people have taught me and who encouraged me. My dad was great! He was a quiet man. My mother was louder in her encouragements."

I was on a cable television show in Oceanside, California, as a professional talking about child abuse. At that time, I was a manager. I was able to go on television and talk about the mental issues of children. So, I thought it was cool that our big department head allowed me to represent our program and the issue of child abuse."

"My biggest acknowledgment was my licensure. At work and church, Christ has always been at the center of my life, because I had such a good experience growing up in my church in Chicago. My parents were both active. My dad was in the Holy Name Society, and my mom was helping out, too. She made the pancake breakfast; she and her best friend in church. We would all be working together. We did a lot of programs for the church. So, it's always been a part of my life."

"When we moved to California and I started going to St. Patrick's church, I started finding young adult groups to attend. From the start, I was always doing something, like a Confraternity of Christian Doctrine (CCD) teacher of middle school. This is popularly known as the "Catechism." I was the coordinator of the young adult ministry and I became a Eucharistic Minister to the home bound and I helped start up the Mental Health Ministry (MHM) group. I said, "We'll start it but we have to trust the Holy Spirit to blow it where it's going to go. We're not in charge of that. Now, the Holy Spirit is blowing everywhere."

"Through all this, God is always there. He is in this whole thing. I remember I was not even working at Rady's yet. I was working in an inpatient psychiatric hospital. My boss said, "Virginia, Balboa Hospital needs someone to talk to the parents. The kids are ages zero to five." I said, okay, and I started reading about kids ages zero to five. What do I know about zero to five children? I am not even licensed yet! So, I've already read everything that I could find. In the middle of the night, I'm trying to go to sleep, and in neon green words – Biting. I got up and started reading about it."

"The nurse at Balboa, who walked me through the doors, said, "We're so happy you're here because they have such a problem with biting." It's been like that every time I've asked for guidance."

"There was another time when I was working on a different residential program and I felt I needed to get something for a certain kid. I was looking for a certain poster at Target. I couldn't find it and I said, "Lord, please help me find it. It's just for this kid. It would be so special to him." I went back and I found the poster that I was looking for. It was not here a minute ago, but "Thank you."

"One of my challenges is that I'm a marriage and family therapist, but I'm not married. I don't even have any kids. What is this, God? You put me in this position, and I'm helping a lot of other parents, but I'm not walking that walk, myself. And, my friend, Lisa, said, "You know what, Virginia, you've been a spiritual mother for a lot of these kids, and you've been a mother-figure for a lot of the other parents." I haven't thought about it that way. Now, I'm parenting my own mother."

8.4 *Let Me Take You Along in My Little Yellow Jeepney!*

Jocelyn, a Licensed Clinical Psychologist, said she always knew she wanted to work with children. During her elementary years, she wanted to become a teacher like many in her family.

In high school, she observed her peers engage in delinquent behaviors, which resulted in severe consequences, such as being sentenced to juvenile hall. After being released, these peers engaged in the same delinquent behaviors. These incidents picked her curiosity. She said,

"Typically, after consequences, individuals modify and/or change their behavior. I was perplexed! From that moment on, I knew I wanted to study human behavior to understand the function of people's behaviors."

"In my Post-doctorate, I worked with children and adolescents centering on the neurodiverse population in diagnosing and assessing for learning exceptionalities. I used children's picture books to help teach socio-emotional learning and social communication skills, which sparked my interest in someday writing my own."

"Little Yellow Jeepney initially started as the first Filipino children's book I wrote and evolved into an independent publishing company in which several other books grew including the language series that teaches children basic Filipino."

"Little Yellow Jeepney has sold over five thousand books. It is heart-warming to see the impact of our books and the important role it plays in cultural appreciation and promoting the preservation of the Filipino language."

I asked her how sharing her God-given talents, skills, and wisdom changed people's lives for the better. She said, "It's really rewarding to hear from clients about how therapy has helped them feel more confident, hopeful, and empowered."

"In therapy, I am thankful to my clients for trusting me to hold space for them and allowing me to help them give some distance between what they are currently thinking and feeling, to understand what is happening to them. It is important to help them realize that self-criticism is a story they are weaving about themselves and that the story can be changed. I have deep respect for those who are willing to seek help during difficult times in their lives."

Her advice to people who would like to follow the life path that she has chosen is: "The traditional education system might not be the perfect fit for everyone. The good news is success has many definitions and paths! I was lucky to discover my passion early, but it's not the only way to find fulfillment. I believe that you define your success and get to create the path to achieve it. Success isn't linear. There are many ways to achieve your goals, so do not feel limited by just one option. Explore your interest. Keep an open mind and know that you are not meant to only do one thing." Well done, Dr. Joy! Thank you.

The fame and reputation gua is responsible for nurturing recognition, self-expression, and creativity. By activating this area, you can enhance your reputation, improve relationships with others, and create a supportive environment that fosters confidence and self-promotion.

The fame and reputation gua is located in the rear middle section of your home. It is directly opposite the career/life path gua. You can bring a little bit of black, gray, or midnight blue to this area to help you figure out what your life's purpose is. Then, it would make it easier for you to self-promote.

The element that resides in this gua is fire. A fireplace would be the best object to put in this area. You can also put a bonfire here, maybe outside.

Hang or display diplomas, certificates, trophies, letters of recommendation, and acknowledgment.

8.5 Four Pillars of Destiny or Bazi: Birthday Readings

This is an ancient Chinese astrological system used to analyze an individual's birth date and time of birth to gain insights into their destiny, personality, strengths, and weaknesses. It is based on the principles of Taoism and the five elements.

BaZi is used for various purposes, such as:

1. Self-discovery and personal growth.
2. Career guidance and planning.
3. Relationship compatibility analysis.
4. Understanding one's life purpose and destiny.

While BaZi has its roots in Chinese culture, its principles and applications are universal, offering valuable insights to anyone interested in exploring their birth chart and life path.

8.6 Home/Business Readings

In Feng Shui, the "commanding position" refers to the optimal placement of furnitures and positioning oneself in a space to achieve a sense of safety, stability, and prosperity. This positioning is typically characterized by:

1. Placing furniture in a diagonal line from the door creates a sense of stability and support.
2. Positioning yourself with your back to a solid wall or a sturdy structure, symbolizing support and protection.
3. Having a clear view of the door, but not directly in line with it, to feel safe and secure.
4. Being able to see the entire room, but not being in a direct line with the door to feel in control. By adopting the commanding position in your home or business, you can:

- Improve your sense of security and stability.
- Enhance your productivity and focus. Boost your confidence and decision-making abilities.
- Enjoy better relationships and communication.
- Increase your overall well-being and prosperity.

The commanding position is all about finding a balance between feeling safe and secure while also being able to see opportunities and possibilities.

Lyn Fernandez
Feng Shui
Interior Design
Northwind
Feng Shui
Consulting
(760) 224-3186
northwind168@sbcglobal.net
www.northwindfengshui.com
Align & activate your space to welcome opportunities and prosperity (home/business floorplan required)
Birthday reading for health, career, personality, compatibilities